ACTIVE INVESTING

Take Charge of your Portfolio in
Today's Unpredictable Markets

Peter Sander, M.B.A.

Adams Media
Avon, Massachusetts

Copyright ©2005 Peter Sander.
All rights reserved. This book, or parts thereof, may not be reproduced in any form without permission from the publisher; exceptions are made for brief excerpts used in published reviews.

Published by
Adams Media, an F+W Publications Company
57 Littlefield Street, Avon, MA 02322. U.S.A.
www.adamsmedia.com

ISBN: 1-59337-282-5

Printed in Canada.

J I H G F E D C B A

Library of Congress Cataloging-in-Publication Data
Sander, Peter
Active investing / Peter Sander.
p. cm.
ISBN 1-59337-282-5
1. Investments—Handbooks, manuals, etc. I. Title.
HG4527.S23 2005
332.6—dc22
                  2004026845

This publication is designed to provide accurate and authoritative information with regard to the subject matter covered. It is sold with the understanding that the publisher is not engaged in rendering legal, accounting, or other professional advice. If legal advice or other expert assistance is required, the services of a competent professional person should be sought.
    —From a *Declaration of Principles* jointly adopted by a Committee of the American Bar Association and a Committee of Publishers and Associations

Many of the designations used by manufacturers and sellers to distinguish their products are claimed as trademarks. Where those designations appear in this book and Adams Media was aware of a trademark claim, the designations have been printed with initial capital letters.

Screenshots on pages 171, 173, 175, 176, 178, and 179 were reproduced with permission of Yahoo! Inc. © 2004 by Yahoo! Inc. YAHOO! and the YAHOO! logo are trademarks of Yahoo! Inc.

Interior illustrations by Argosy.

This book is available at quantity discounts for bulk purchases.
For information, please call 1-800-872-5627.

Contents

Introduction . . . . *v*

Part I: The Active Investing Imperative

Chapter 1:   Lessons Learned: How We Got Here *3*

Chapter 2:   The Investing Climate: Changed Forever *15*

Chapter 3:   What Is Active Investing? *31*

Part II: The Informed and Equipped Active Investor

Chapter 4:   Windows to the Investing World *49*

Chapter 5:   Through the Window:
             What Active Investors Look For. *65*

Chapter 6:   Executing Your Strategy:
             Platforms for Active Investors *73*

Chapter 7:   Economic Indicators and the
             Business Cycle. *83*

Part III: The Quest for Value

Chapter 8: Value Investing for Today's Investor *103*

Chapter 9: Appraising a Business: A Value Approach . . . *113*

Part IV: Trading Tools and Techniques for Active Investors

Chapter 10: Playing for the Short Term *149*

Chapter 11: Signs of Opportunity *163*

Chapter 12: Buying and Selling *181*

Part V: Blending Investments and Investing Styles

Chapter 13: Fund Investing for Active Investors *193*

Chapter 14: Investing Potpourri: Specialized Tools for Both Sides of the Market *213*

Chapter 15: Putting Active Investing into Practice: Principles and Examples. *239*

Index *257*

Introduction

Where were you in 2002? Like a combat experience, we all went through it and most survived, but we all have bad memories. Most of us hid under a rock as the markets tumbled to their lows, as much as 80 percent off of their 2000 highs. The NASDAQ closed at 1114.73 on October 9, 2002, down nearly 4000 points from its March 2000 high. The investing casualty list was long. Many investors lost their savings and even their 401(k)s, and many more of those fortunate enough to have anything left to invest found their safe haven in real estate or some other "basic" investment. Then there were the fortunate ones who saw the debacle coming. Though their moves seemed awkward or even downright wrong at the time, they came out smelling like a rose by selling stocks and buying bonds, dreary real estate trusts, utilities, or other "boring" investments. In hindsight, wouldn't we all have liked to have been so boring?

But most of us simply took cover. We pondered our investing lives and wondered why. We owned the right investments—didn't we? We allocated our assets, listened to the professionals, bought and held, owned Cisco and Microsoft, dollar-cost-averaged, and all of that. We still got creamed. Those that simply "bought the market" through conventional mutual and index funds lost 20 to 40 percent. More aggressive investors lost much more. Companies went bankrupt; executives cooked the books; analysts abused investment banking relationships, and entire industries like telecom, utilities, and consumer photography changed forever. What was once trusted could be trusted no longer. Never before in our investing lives had we felt so out of control, with such a strong feeling that external events and market turmoil controlled our investments. We moved from the comfort and simplicity of smooth-air flight to a horrific scenario requiring rapid-fire active piloting of an airplane in the center of a storm. What changed?

As Warren Buffett once said, "When the tide goes out we see who's been swimming naked." Holy cow, did a lot of unattractive flesh come into view. Overly aggressive, confident, complacent investors failed to take cover and were exposed. But more than that, as the middle years of the "ought" (2000–2009) decade unfold, investors find many once-venerable investing institutions milling around in their birthday suits. The failings of many financial analysts and brokerage firms started to become apparent in 1999–2000, even as the momentum continued upward. Then, as things started to wash out in 2001, the naked truths of corporate accounting fraud and mutual fund shenanigans came to light. Everyone began to wonder: When you can't trust brokers, analysts, financial advisors, corporate executives, professional money managers, and investment companies, whom *can* you trust?

Time for a disclaimer: Finding a few bad apples doesn't mean you should throw out the whole barrel with them. Clearly not all brokers or analysts or executives or fund managers are dishonest; clearly not all corporate books are cooked. Nevertheless, these events serve as a collective wakeup call that you, the owner of your assets and the manager of your future, cannot just throw everything over the wall for someone else to worry about, while you never think about it again. Those investment assets are yours, and you must think and act strategically, playing both defense and offense to win in the long term.

Introduction

Status Quo No More

For better or for worse, it's a changed and rapidly evolving playing field we are moving on, likely for the rest of our investing lives. The easy money was made—and lost—as more and more novice and unwitting investors came into the markets and fed their assets to the monster. But more than that, many tried-and-true investing paradigms found their way to the trash heap. We heard the old standards of buy-and-hold, no-load mutual funds, dollar cost averaging, "buy on 10 percent pullbacks" on every radio show, *Wall Street Week*, and new investing book (and there were a lot of them) from the 1990s. In addition to these rather plain vanilla strategies, we heard about the more exotic day trading, swing trading, "sure thing" options trading, technical analysis, IPOs, and others.

Everyone knows that the "anything goes" party climaxed in a glittering crescendo in March of 2000. No single event sparked the change, and many disagree when the status quo really started to melt away. But as it did, events served to accelerate it dramatically: first, the meltdown of Enron, MCI, Adelphia Communications, and other once "solid" investments, and second, the events of September 11, 2001, which accelerated the exit of weak hands from the market and turned the markets into something to "come back to" with greater care and precision.

As the "ought" decade unfolds, people are realizing what they "ought"—and ought not—do. Successful investors have learned that they must *manage* their own future—though they may *delegate* some of the tasks to someone else.

The demise of blind trust is not the only new paradigm. Lower expected returns on investments present a huge challenge. The 15 to 20 percent annual returns enjoyed from 1995–2000 were an anomaly, if for no other reason than that the economy at large as measured by Gross Domestic Product (GDP) was growing at a more modest 3 to 5 percent per year. Sure, some factors may support a climate where investments grow at a faster rate—at least for a while—than the economy as a whole. These include the greater concentration of business activity and wealth in market-traded players (example: Wal-Mart replacing small stores) as well as greater profitability through productivity and efficiency (it's not just the amount of business, it's profits that ultimately count). There is no doubt that business will continue to concentrate and the big will survive. Nevertheless, economists and investment professionals unanimously see more modest investment returns in the future, generally in the range of 4 to 8 percent per year. And as we'll see, a more modest return—even 1 to 2 percent less—means a much smaller nest egg over the long haul.

With this series of complex factors in mind, *Active Investing—Take Charge of Your Portfolio in Today's Unpredictable Markets* is a new approach for today's investor. Active investing, as defined here, blends the best of several investing styles and vehicles for *today's busy investor*. The active investing style is enlightened, rooted in sound business rationale, versatile, and, at least in part, a do-it-yourself enterprise.

Active investing isn't day trading, value investing, nor any other "pure" strategy. It isn't exclusive to options trading, mutual fund switching, swing trading, or technical analysis. It's a blend of information, tools, and techniques from each of these arenas. Today's savvy investor blends investing styles, vehicles, and time horizons, and plays both sides of the market. For those who still want professional help, blended investing may include a mix of professional advice and self-management. To get closer to the idea, let's examine key words in the title:

Active

Active investors watch markets daily
foundational base of long-term investm
active portfolio segments looking for
and changes in market leadership. Acti
the economic, market, and business news that affects their invest-
ments. Most do research at least weekly. Active investors build a margin of safety and create short-term income through derivative investments such as equity and index options. The *versatile* active investor employs a *blend* of investment tools and vehicles to his strategic advantage.

Investing

The active *investor* is not a pure trader or speculator and is most definitely not a gambler. Active investors use solid rationale for their market moves, selecting their market choices based on economic and market forces and internal company specifics. Active *investors* know value and how to spot it in the marketplace both for short- and long-term investments.

. . . for Today's Unpredictable Markets

Business and markets change, often literally at the speed of light. Business cycles are getting shorter and shorter, and at no time in the past has "buy and hold" appeared so dangerous. Railroads were "glamor" investments for seventy years; radio lasted twenty years, and the Internet just three. It's no surprise that Bill Gates' main defense of the Microsoft monopoly hinged on the notion that today's Windows monopoly might be outmoded in just five years. Who would have predicted the rapid demise of photo film and Kodak twenty, or even ten years ago? Or what's happened to traditional copper-wire phone service? Today's active

ACTIVE INVESTING

stays aware of short- and long-term market trends and s. They must change investments to fit the times, take their rofits, and hedge against the worst. They must learn to "stay on top of the bull" no matter which way it bolts.

Active investors are experienced, but not professional investors. Though they've found that managing their own investments is the best strategy, they don't want to spend day and night tracking markets and doing research. Whether endowed with substantial assets to protect and grow or just starting out, active investors want to take charge with a sound do-it-yourself investing strategy and thought process. Sound like you? Read on.

Part I:

The Active Investing Imperative

Chapter 1

Lessons Learned: How We Got Here

The dramatic developments of the last five to seven years are not an isolated event or one-time "speed bump" on the road to wealth accumulation. The causes of the "bubble" and its collapse should be looked at in the broader context of the business, financial, and social climate of recent years. Business and regulatory change, exacerbated by technology, social change, vastly increased market participation, and dependence from a growing set of players has brought about true change in the investing climate. Together, all of these events have shaped the new investing imperative for the twenty-first century—a more active investing style. The "storm" of 2000–2003 is not by itself unique; others have occurred nearly every decade during the past 150 years. But the rapid pace of business change, greater financial self-determinism (we can't just sit back and wait for the pension to kick in), and the better tools available to the investing public all call for a different response this time. To understand today's investing, you first must take a look at the "big picture" of the last fifty years.

The "Good Old Days"—the 1950s and '60s

Time was, you simply bought the market. You plunked down hard-earned money to invest in the American Way, believing it to be the best and most economically progressive way on the planet. You owned General Motors, General Mills, RCA, and, if a little more aggressive, IBM or Xerox. The stock certificates sat in your safety deposit box, and you most likely only called your broker if you had accumulated a little more money to invest, or if some was needed for a major purchase. A few government bonds or savings bonds may have sat alongside the stock certificates, purchased as much out of patriotic duty as for safety or investment return. Maybe a bank or S&L CD was purchased with an eye for safety but also for the kitchen appliance "premium."

You checked the paper at most weekly. At that time many major newspapers didn't have stock tables, as you were among the mere 20 percent of the population that owned investments. You watched the Dow Industrials, Rails, Utilities, 65 Stocks on the nightly *Huntley-Brinkley* report. You cared more about the averages than your individual stocks, for the market *was* your stocks. There was no "NASDAQ," and "Over The Counter" stocks were a murky unknown world mostly to be avoided. You probably bought stock in companies you worked for, and you also bought the company's products out of a sense of duty to support *your* business. Your investments grew with the economy. There was little to worry about—and little for you to do.

Political Ties and International Dependence—the 1970s

After the stock markets hit their then-all-time peak in 1972 (the Dow even exceeded 1000 points for a short period), they came unglued in a hurry with events leading up to the OPEC oil embargo of 1973–74. The economy, taxed by the sudden hike in oil prices, wasn't growing any more, and investments tumbled almost 50 percent over the next year and a half. Investors—and there still weren't many with large market stakes—had to start paying attention. The "nifty fifty" blue chip and glamor stocks of the day were no longer a sure thing. Hidden among the myriad other news items affecting the investing world were two important status quo changes in the investing industry with lasting impact.

The Arrival of NASDAQ

In 1971, NASDAQ (which stands for National Association of Securities Dealers Automated Quotations) arrived on the scene. NASDAQ provided the first real-time open market where dealers could post quotes visible to all dealers with electronic order routing. For the first time, dealers—and to a degree, individual investors—could see what everyone in the market was doing. The market for these stocks went from being controlled by a few players to being controlled by no one in particular, a major step toward democratizing the markets and gaining easy access for the individual investor.

May Day: Commission Deregulation

On May 1, 1975, high fixed brokerage commissions became a thing of the past. A more competitive environment evolved with more, better, and cheaper services for individual investors. But perhaps more importantly, commission deregulation reduced market friction. Smaller commissions allowed more investors to trade in and out of stocks more frequently without worrying about high fixed commission costs. Markets became dramatically more liquid, with more orders in the pile. Shifts between stock sectors, as well as in and out of the market, became much more feasible.

In the 1970s investors and investment professionals alike started to realize that investments weren't bound to follow the economy as a whole, that certain sectors and industries were bound to do better than others. Cyclical companies and companies overly dependent on cheap, abundant resources—such as foreign oil—were no longer the best bets. It was certainly the beginning of a more complex, dynamic investing climate with an ever-expanding list of factors that influenced investing performance. The advent of NASDAQ and deregulated commissions made "Main Street" do-it-yourself investing really feasible for the first time.

Globalization, Asset Shift, and Technology— the 1980s

Aside from the oil embargo and the two major equity market changes noted, the 1970s were fairly uneventful. The Dow Jones Industrial average traded in a modest 500-point range through the decade. Businesses, dogged by political uncertainty, high interest rates, high commodity prices, and general inflation couldn't get much traction in those days. "Stagflation" became the buzzword of the day. Key industries like automobiles and steel now had to deal with foreign competition. There were few individual investors in the market, and most new entrants came in through the mutual fund route, one just starting to gain popularity due to its simplicity, trading cost edge for very small investors, and professional managers able to understand the ever more complex business world.

Ronald Reagan took office in January 1980 with little market fanfare—at least initially. However, the high interest rates at the time (at one point the Fed discount rate was 22 percent—compare that to the 1 percent-plus rates of 2003–04!) stifled any business growth and convinced most that hard assets such as real estate—though expensive to buy—were still the best choices for asset ownership. Interest rates were kept artificially high just to combat inflation, and businesses paid the price in two ways—high interest rates *and* high commodity prices. The inflation factor became the biggest "swing factor" in most business decisions.

As August 1982 approached, interest rates had started downward and inflation had started to subside. President Reagan pushed through tax legislation that included a new assortment of retirement savings incentives for individuals and small businesses. Transportation deregulation, more free trade, and increased government spending in the technology and defense sectors added to the story. The result was a long-awaited shift of capital from real estate and fixed assets into stocks. The "bull run," which was to last almost eighteen years with a few short interruptions, had begun.

Helped out by the new retirement savings initiatives, the newly rediscovered stock market grew steadily through the mid-1980s. Suddenly, picking stocks was cool again, and exciting developments in technology and computers made "playing the market" a sport available to the masses.

A Perfect Storm

As the decade went on, the market continued upward to a point more than triple its modest August 1982 beginnings—at least until one horrible day in October 1987. Lower taxes, as well as business and consumer optimism, had led the markets higher and induced people to spend more in their personal lives as well. But what were they buying? A lot of foreign goods. Buying foreign had become cool not only for cars but also for everything else from clothes, food, and skis to home décor, tires, and beer.

A ballooning trade deficit resulted, and in order to keep the dollar relatively strong and attractive for foreign investment, interest rates were kept high. The leftover inflation fear from a few years back also fueled a lingering high interest rate mentality. That week in 1987, a particularly bad trade deficit report, high interest rates of more than 10 percent for U.S. Treasury bonds, a period of almost uninterrupted stock market growth, and some speculative excess in stocks like Digital Equipment created a volatile mix. On Monday, October 19, 1987, the Dow dropped from more than 2700 points to just above 2200—the worst one-day percentage plunge ever.

The situation was made worse by the increased participation of novice individual investors and the fact that investing infrastructure had not evolved to handle such an event. Most buy and sell orders were manual or at best semi-automated. The resulting onslaught of orders overburdened the system and caused requests to sell (or buy) to be ignored altogether, adding to the panic.

Shocked investors lost their proverbial shirts. A lot of wealth disappeared, and what was left seemed to be teetering on the brink. Everyone watched the overseas markets with bated breath. Would they rush to cash in their U.S. investments and debt securities? Many investors—with good reason—woke up to realize that some of their wealth had disappeared into the coffers of Japan, Hong Kong, or Singapore. For the first time, U.S. market results might be dictated by what happened to the Nikkei, the Hang Seng, and the German DAX. People watched the newly available CNN around the clock, waiting to see what signals these markets would send. Now it felt like the stock market was never closed—it just shifted to different parts of the world through the day.

Fortunately, foreign investors stood pat and did nothing to exacerbate the crisis. The Fed followed by pumping the system with liquidity and by gradually reducing interest rates. After a six-month consolidation period, investors once again gained confidence and started back in again, but this time more cautiously.

Business, aided by technology, was changing faster. Government policy was also changing faster, and for the first time really being used to prop up asset values. Even the most secure long-term investor now had to watch for such "perfect storms" that could wipe out huge chunks of market value. Conditions were still favorable for investing in businesses—and even more so as interest rates and the dollar declined. But the imperative to stay aware of what was going on—and at least somewhat active—grew by leaps and bounds during this event.

Technology, Democratization, and the Internet Bubble—the 1990s

Saddam Hussein kicked off the 1990s with his invasion of Kuwait in September 1990 and the resulting "Gulf War I" that followed. The markets held their breath. By March 1991, we could all breath easily again. But while the markets initially applauded the end of the threat, an extended period of economic dislocation still followed. The boom of the 1980s had gotten tired; key industries such as autos and basic manufacturing saw a down cycle, exacerbated once again by the flood of imports. The markets really didn't get going again until 1992—an election year. A youthful Bill Clinton and his vision of the "information superhighway" jazzed the markets, particularly the technology sector. The vision promised faster, more efficient business and a new conduit to reach customers. Few knew what the Internet really was at that point, but it sounded pretty good.

Within a couple of short years after Clinton's inauguration, the first fruits of the vision started to show. Americans could sign up on America Online. Businesses could network their computers and operations with each other, and e-mail became a standard within corporate walls. The growth of the Internet was not just a boon to suppliers of Internet "parts" and to new Internet-only companies building a new channel to sell old products. It also was a new opportunity for all businesses to build a new market presence and streamline or simplify operations. Every company developed a "web strategy" and executed it, at least some of it, in record time. The stock market liked what it saw and recognized all companies, both suppliers and beneficiaries, of this new exciting business paradigm.

In 1995 and 1996 supply started to catch up with demand in certain "hot" industry sectors such as Internet hardware and the memory chips required to make personal computers. An enduring law of business (known to supply chain managers as the "dreaded diamond effect") holds that supply will catch up with—and usually surpass—demand for any "hot" product, particularly when there had been an earlier shortage, and particularly when cheap foreign supply is likely to enter the market. As supply increases, concern about unfulfilled orders eases, and many "just in case" orders are canceled—thus exacerbating the transition to oversupply, price cuts, and reduced profits. This was clearly happening with memory chips, disrupting the business performance of chip suppliers as well as the suppliers of materials for that industry such as capital equipment, test instruments, design software, specialty chemicals, etc. Such dislocations may be confined to one sector; however, they can spill over into the whole market and economy. We saw it again five years later with telecommunications and networking equipment. These events added more evidence that market players needed to track short-term business conditions within their invested industries.

There were more speed bumps in the late 1990s. In 1997, a currency crisis created by poor monetary policy in the rapidly growing Asian nations caused another short but sharp market decline. A crisis mentality took hold again in the fall of 1998 when Russia defaulted on some international debt. These sharp declines were driven by fear and world events; most of all, they occurred because stocks needed a breather and people had a reason to sell.

In June of 1998, the stock price of a small company called Amazon.com started to move. Suddenly the market got hold of the dot.com idea, and the stock rocketed skyward. Soon other companies began to follow suit. The whole game became finding companies that hadn't been "found" yet and buying them before they took off. This strategy worked most of the time, egged on by huge initial public offering (IPO) run-ups for still more companies and the beginnings of a merger phase. The Internet stock boom took the rest of the market with it. Like most booms, there was some rationale—the cost of doing business would go down, sales would go up, and everyone would march happily to the bank.

This notion of business utopia combined with stock market excitement to create a self-fulfilling prophecy. The notion that things were getting better made things better. But there was still another force at work—one shaped by the Internet. For the first time in history, individual investors had virtual real-time connections to the stock market. Free and easy access gave entry to many more market players, and the market was already in a boom to begin with . . .

In the late 1990s the last overhanging concern—and in some cases, source of paranoia—was the year 2000—and what that particular number would mean to the computer code now running everything. The reality: Years of preparation and purchase of new equipment made "Y2K" a nonevent. The one legacy that Y2K had created was huge demand for technology products—so much so that businesses woke up in January 2000 and soon started wondering where all the business had gone. At the same time, the huge capital inflow into the markets from individual investors and venture capitalists started to play out as people began to wonder when they would start getting a return on their investments.

Once again, a perfect storm was brewing. This time it wasn't global events or interest rates—it was a fading business cycle and the realization that, while the Internet brought improvements in business productivity, it wasn't an "off the charts" improvement. The use of the Internet did not guarantee success. The Internet was a tool to execute a sound business strategy, not a business strategy in itself.

The grim result and profound lessons are recent enough to stick in the minds of all investors. There were many lessons—some repeated from history and some new. Among the lessons learned:

- No bull market can go on forever.
- Overvalued stocks are indeed valued above their worth and should be treated as such.
- Growth in value of business assets cannot consistently exceed growth in the economy.
- It takes more than a business plan to guarantee success.

One other obvious realization from this period: Business cycles are becoming ever shorter, and investors need to stay on top of these cycles and invest accordingly. As the years 2001 and 2002 began to unfold, investors came to realize that the "perfect storm" of the millennium was more powerful than anyone thought.

Trust Shattered and All Things Reconsidered —the "Oughts"

As this "perfect storm" began to blow, other events began to release their fury on the investment world, events that would shake the very foundation of "traditional" investment behavior and practice and that would make the vastly grown pool of individual investors once again wary of the markets.

The fallout started in late 2000 with persistent downward momentum in the markets. Earnings results were at best flat; sales forecasts released by major companies were flat or even declining. Clearly the business cycle had shifted and had started to contract with reduced demand, reduced inventories, and canceled orders. The message had changed from steadily rising expectations to executive bewilderment, lack of "visibility," and a strongly implied "things won't be what they were for a long time," and investor confidence was spooked with predictable results.

In November 2001, Enron shocked the investment world with a revelation of a $1 *billion* writeoff for assets suddenly were deemed worthless. No longer could we trust what had been sacred—the reporting of financial results. When Adelphia Communications and the still more mainstream WorldCom went down for much the same reason, we suddenly realized a much bigger problem. Most individuals—and a large number of professional investors and analysts, for that matter—never really understood financial statements. We had forgotten that while assets might be fictitious and subjectively valued, liabilities are always real. Following the trail of how a company came up with its numbers was nearly impossible, and in the era of increased public visibility, where any earnings "miss" was sure to be punished, executives did what they could to make things look right. Investors knew the books could be cooked but were surprised by how much.

Meanwhile, questions started to emerge about the brokerage and investment banking industries. The very companies who hired these analysts and published their advice had investment banking relationships with companies they followed. If a firm had loaned millions to a company and was making millions more selling that company's securities to investors, under what circumstances would that firm tell the public that investing in that company was a bad idea? Not many. Fewer than 10 percent of all analysts had recommendations to sell any stock.

Beyond that, the boom had attracted hundreds of thousands into the business of selling securities as investment advisors, brokers, and other investment "professionals." Brokerage and financial services firms were chasing the growing numbers of potential clients. Financial services firms at the periphery—credit unions, banks, and insurance agencies—all wanted to get into the action, and they hired anyone who could wear a tie, take a test, and get a license. Quantity replaced quality in the financial services business, and many investors lost out. Some lost out even more when incompetence gave way to dishonesty, as many of these intermediaries overhyped and overtraded questionable securities to fatten their own take.

Then—as if it weren't enough not to be able to trust corporate accounting, corporate executives, and traditional financial services firms—the mutual fund industry dropped yet another bomb. Who would have thought that mutual funds, the time-honored, dignified bastions of "Main Street" investing would have, behind the scenes, been fleecing millions of average investors by letting Wall Street insiders trade the funds to their advantage? While seemingly harmless—taking a few tenths of a percent at most—these practices added to already high and questionable fees and charges collected by most funds. The bottom line: Now mutual funds, set up to help protect people from Wall Street in the first place, were added to the growing list of what couldn't be trusted. The inevitable result: Trust tumbled to an all-time low. People either left the market or just went inactive, hoping things would come back.

Chapter 2

The Investing Climate: Changed Forever

It's your choice whether to become (or continue to be) a do-it-yourself investor. You may decide that the world is just too complex to keep up with on your own. Either way, structural changes in business, politics, technology, and trust have exerted profound influence on the investing climate, affecting short- and long-term investment behavior, and ultimately, your investing approach. The *calculus* of these changes is most striking—that is, that they are occurring at a more rapid pace. The changes in business, politics, technology, and trust in the past ten years far exceed those of any prior decade—and there is no slowdown in sight. There has been a major climate shift in investing, with the result that many popular investing strategies and paradigms have become passé or just downright ineffective. The next sections summarize what has changed in today's investment climate and how you should adapt your investment strategy accordingly.

Technology

The Internet drove an investing technology revolution in the 1990s. Cheap, real-time market access and the instantaneous dissemination of information brought about by the Internet have changed investing forever. *Disintermediation*—the elimination of middlemen spotlighted during the growing phases of the Internet boom—will probably rise to enjoy another heyday in service industries like retail and insurance. Even more, technologically stable businesses are applying technology to streamline manufacturing, marketing, and customer support processes. The point: Technology is affecting all industries and all markets. Investors often fail to appreciate technology change in even the most stable industries.

Today's investor must understand the businesses and industries they invest in. The effect of technology on processes, products, and services is a big part of that picture. Is the company keeping up (or leading) in releasing the latest technologies in its products? Is it keeping up (or leading), deploying technology in its own operations? It is hard to know the answers for sure, but it's becoming more important as an investor to develop and confirm a basic awareness. Also, it is not enough for a company to simply *embrace* technology—some firms look at R&D expenditures and the number of patents generated as ends in and of themselves—they must be able to bring these initiatives to market successfully—and profitably.

The Service Economy

The U.S. economic shift from manufacturing to a service-based economy is already familiar to most. But product technology and increased digitization means that economic advantage will shift more and more to companies offering better service with their products and to those that can find better channels in which to distribute them. It is no longer sufficient to sell the best widgets—

they must arrive on time and be ready to use with information and service needed by the customer. Weakness in this area usually forces a business to cut price to stay competitive; with some notable exceptions, being the price leader is seldom a viable long-term strategy.

The Smaller World of Globalization

Like it or not, the world is becoming a more singular economic entity. Manufacturing is shifting overseas to Asia and Latin America to capture the advantage of lower labor costs. Many players in the service economy will do the same. North America will still be the center of ideas and intellectual property for some time, but economic advantage will accrue to those businesses ahead of the curve in finding the lowest cost structures. Savvy investors follow these trends and keep a close eye on global markets and business patterns. This doesn't necessarily mean that all investors should invest in foreign companies. Instead, they should track how their businesses, U.S.–based or otherwise, perform in the world market. Does the company have an international business, and, if so, do their products sell overseas? Is the brand recognized and supported? Can the company derive benefit from sourcing material, manufactured goods, or services overseas, and, if so, do they? Does the company depend too much on foreign economies or resources? Is the company vulnerable to unfavorable geopolitical events? It all becomes part of the savvy investor's checklist.

Greater Market Participation

The technology changes have already been identified, and more people are forced by the increasingly do-it-yourself nature of retirement planning to manage their investments. Markets will have more players for the foreseeable future. This benefits investing by leveling the playing field and reducing the opportunity for insider manipulation, but it also makes for stronger swings and fluctuations in the market.

Shorter Business Cycles

It took seventy years for the railroad industry to start, build, overbuild, mature, consolidate, and begin its decline. The Internet industry did the same in about seven years. In the case of railroads, technology (highways and trucks) combined with poor management to spearhead the fall. The Internet industry was a victim of overinflated expectations, inexperienced management, and overestimated changes in consumer preferences. In both cases, the industries did not disappear but instead retrenched and found their niches (coal and intermodal hauling for the railroads, while only time will tell for the Internet). The jury is still out on how photography or telecom or computer or the electric utility industries will evolve, but investors must watch these cycles and track the big picture for industries they invest in.

Government Involvement

Back in the early 1970s, fewer than 20 percent of U.S. households invested in the stock market. Today that figure exceeds 50 percent. Politics and public policy have recognized that more people have more money in the markets. Thus the monetary policy of the Federal Reserve Board increasingly does what's good for the market. Election year cycles are stronger than ever, as vote-grabbing tax packages and government spending programs hit the markets. Today's investor must watch Washington and keep close track of economic and political indicators that shape the market's actions.

The Changing Tax Climate

Tax law changes in the 1990s tilted the table toward long-term investing by reducing capital gains taxes on assets held for longer than a year. The more recent 2003 tax change passed by the Bush administration reduced taxes on certain kinds of dividends, thereby raising total return on dividend-paying stocks going forward. Such changes will likely continue and put certain groups of investments in or out of favor.

Greater Volatility

Market volatility has been a common news phrase, and indeed securities markets have become more volatile. Some facts: The stock market, as measured by the Standard & Poor's 500 Index, rose or declined more than 10 percent in each of nine years through 2003, while doing so in only four of the nine years before that. The NASDAQ Composite Index, a measure of the relatively more volatile, technology-intense NASDAQ market, saw a more than 20 percent change either way in each of the same nine years, compared to only once in the previous nine years. Why? Technology change creates faster and stronger industry shifts, faster markets, and more participants. Global interdependence amplifies world political and economic events, and the fast pace of life and media bombardment create changes in both consumer and investor preferences and tastes. These factors work in concert to create a bumpier ride.

Crisis in Confidence:
The Financial Services Industry

The investment boom and diversification of key financial services players brought on a boom in numbers of financial professionals. This appears to have increased the numbers of investment "professionals" but reduced their quality. Short-term focus on generating commissions and fees replaced sound long-term planning principles. While a new movement toward fee-based planning has created more unbiased thinking and a greater selling agnosticism among a few planners, the system is still tied too much to commission selling and half-baked ideas. In today's landscape it is more important than ever to keep tabs on the credentials, approach, and actions of anyone working on your behalf. How are they paid? Do they benefit most from growing your assets? Or selling a particular family of mutual funds? Do they provide sound fundamental rationale for their actions? The list goes on—most people ask more questions to a prospective house painter than they do to their personal financial advisor.

Crisis in Confidence: Accounting Standards and Corporate Governance

Not being able to trust a financial statement is like not being able to trust a resume, a report card, or an aircraft manifest. Misleading financial statements are worse than worthless, for they give us the impression that things are right *and* that we investors know what we're doing. Fortunately, the Securities and Exchange Commission (SEC) and the Financial Accounting Standards Board (FASB) have moved toward tighter standards. Still, investors must be wary, and when financial records are studded with footnotes and you walk away feeling that "the more you know, the more you don't know"—look out. When too much power in an organization is concentrated in one individual (for example, when one person is both chairman of the board and CEO)—look out, because the appropriate checks and balances might be lacking. There has been a recent backlash against corporate malfeasance, and previously unchecked corporate power is being curtailed by stronger and more vocal shareholder constituents. People are once again coming to realize that shareholders are the true owners of businesses. The realization that enhancing shareholder value—not executive personal worth—is the real ball game has come to some faster than others. Today's investors are well served to compare business performance to executive compensation and pick only those companies where executive interests are apparently aligned to their own.

Crisis Intensified: The Changing Perception of Mutual Funds

A bigger concern: recent events in the arena of professionally managed investment companies, known to most as mutual funds. Scandals, touched on earlier, exceeded the depth and breadth any of us thought possible. Bad enough, these investments tended to at best perform with the markets and all too often underperformed (70 percent underperformed the S&P 500 broad market gauge.) Bad enough are the high commissions (loads), fees for managing investments (1 to 2 percent for most actively managed funds) and more fees for marketing ("12b-1" fees, charging owners every year for the costs of marketing the same product to other investors). Overtrading and churning portfolios led to mediocre performance through increased trading costs, taxes, and the natural disadvantage of always being a few steps behind the pack. All mutual funds shouldn't be painted with the same bad broad brush, and many firms offer products that are more than appropriate for many investors. But the scenario serves to remind that investors must be watchful of what they do.

Diminishing Returns

Most experts expect markets to perform in line with overall economic growth, which is likely to be moderate through the next few years. It never was reasonable to expect sustained investment returns greater than 10 percent, and today any expectation exceeding 7 or 8 percent is probably suspect. Investments will have to be well managed even to exceed these levels, particularly if mutual funds or other intermediaries are involved and taking their percentage.

Does the expected rate of return make a difference? You bet. Without a lengthy lesson on investing math, the numbers in **Figure 2.1** are telling. This table shows the compounded growth of $100,000 for time intervals ranging from one to forty years, at a rate of return ("growth rate") from 1 percent to 15 percent. A financial advisor promising 10 percent returns is promising a growth in your wealth to $672,750 in twenty years before taxes—a sixfold increase. A more realistic projection of 5 or 6 percent brings $265,330 and $320,714 respectively. A look through the 20 to 25 year columns reveals that a mere 3 percent reduction (say, 8 percent to 5 percent) in expected returns cuts long-term investing performance in half. Moreover, the table underscores the power of compounding and the difference that even minute changes in return rates—like through the recent dividend tax cuts—can make.

The High Cost of Underperformance

While expected returns are becoming more realistic, the price we pay for *underperformance*—and in many cases, professional management—must be considered. If market performance suggests a 5 percent annual return, and you earn 4 percent, how much does that cost? Moreover, what is the impact of aboveboard fees and charges levied by mutual funds, financial planners, or both? The answer is provided in **Figure 2.2**.

Suppose you own a portfolio of mutual fund investments that earns 6 percent before fees and charges. The funds take a 1 percent management fee and another 0.5 percent "12b-1," or marketing, fee out of what they earn, leaving you with 4.5 percent. Over 25 years, you would have had $429,187 at 6 percent, but the 1.5 percent reduction leaves you with only $300,543—more than one-third of your potential worth. That may be a high price to

The Investing Climate: Changed Forever 23

Figure 2.1: Compounded Growth of $100,000

Growth Rate	1	2	5	10	15	20	25	30	40
1.0%	$101,000	$102,010	$105,101	$110,462	$116,097	$122,019	$128,243	$134,785	$148,886
2.0%	$102,000	$104,040	$110,408	$121,899	$134,587	$148,595	$164,061	$181,136	$220,804
3.0%	$103,000	$106,090	$115,927	$134,392	$155,797	$180,611	$209,378	$242,726	$326,204
4.0%	$104,000	$108,160	$121,665	$148,024	$180,094	$219,112	$266,584	$324,340	$480,102
5.0%	$105,000	$110,250	$127,628	$162,889	$207,893	$265,330	$338,635	$432,194	$703,999
6.0%	$106,000	$112,360	$133,823	$179,085	$239,656	$320,714	$429,187	$574,349	$1,028,572
7.0%	$107,000	$114,490	$140,255	$196,715	$275,903	$386,968	$542,743	$761,226	$1,497,446
8.0%	$108,000	$116,640	$146,933	$215,892	$317,217	$466,096	$684,848	$1,006,266	$2,172,452
9.0%	$109,000	$118,810	$153,862	$236,736	$364,248	$560,441	$862,308	$1,326,768	$3,140,942
10.0%	$110,000	$121,000	$161,051	$259,374	$417,725	$672,750	$1,083,471	$1,744,940	$4,525,926
11.0%	$111,000	$123,210	$168,506	$283,942	$478,459	$806,231	$1,358,546	$2,289,230	$6,500,087
12.0%	$112,000	$125,440	$176,234	$310,585	$547,357	$964,629	$1,700,006	$2,995,992	$9,305,097
13.0%	$113,000	$127,690	$184,244	$339,457	$625,427	$1,152,309	$2,123,054	$3,911,590	$13,278,155
14.0%	$114,000	$129,960	$192,541	$370,722	$713,794	$1,374,349	$2,646,192	$5,095,016	$18,888,351
15.0%	$115,000	$132,250	$201,136	$404,556	$813,706	$1,636,654	$3,291,895	$6,621,177	$26,786,355

Number of Years

Figure 2.2: Cumulative Effect of Market Underperformance

6% Market Return

UNDERPERFORM the Market By	Number of Years:							
	1	2	5	10	15	20	25	30	40
	$106,000	$112,360	$133,823	$179,085	$239,656	$320,714	$429,187	$574,349	$1,028,572
0.5%	$105,500	$111,303	$130,696	$170,814	$223,248	$291,776	$381,339	$498,395	$851,331
1.0%	$105,000	$110,250	$127,628	$162,889	$207,893	$265,330	$338,635	$432,194	$703,999
1.5%	$104,500	$109,203	$124,618	$155,297	$193,528	$241,171	$300,543	$374,532	$581,636
2.0%	$104,000	$108,160	$121,665	$148,024	$180,094	$219,10.12	$266,584	$324,340	$480,102
2.5%	$103,500	$107,123	$118,769	$141,060	$167,535	$198,979	$236,324	$280,679	$395,926

pay for the security and the transfer of effort in having someone else working for you, but it isn't necessarily a bad deal so long as that path is consciously chosen.

At the same time, today's needs and goals make it even more important to keep investing returns strong. It looks ever less likely that government entitlements (such as Social Security) will fund retirement. Corporate pension plans are under fire (although they are still protected by law and government-sponsored insurance). Retirement medical benefits are under fire. You get the point. You're likely to need more, and whether you have it down the road is more than ever up to you. Thus a fundamental theme of this book: A more active investing approach is required to (1) defend against sub-par performance and (2) get returns even slightly above the performance of the economy and its representative markets. Active investing means playing both defense and offense, and it means making your game plan flexible and versatile enough to reap the market's fruits where they grow.

Panaceas No More

The history lessons and climate changes discussed so far show just how much things have changed and how they are still changing rapidly. One lesson: Investors should never "camp" for long periods of time on a single investing idea. "New" investing ideas come and go almost as quickly as main street fads. Why? There are several reasons. First, the landscape of business and investing itself changes. Second, there is a tendency for people to climb on board with certain investing ideas, only to dump them when they stop working. Such ideas look good for a while during the period while everyone else is climbing on board and reading the latest book about the latest sure-fire investing technique. When they play out, look out.

To illustrate this point, consider that there are at least 27,000 books listed on Amazon.com under the category of investing. It is safe to say that most describe a singular investing vehicle or style. Most of the investing advice that you see in other media—radio, TV, newspapers—and in fancy seminars also deals with singular vehicles and investing approaches. Growth stocks, income stocks, defensive stocks, bonds, junk bonds, options, commodities, mutual funds, index funds, exchange-traded funds and currencies are all investing vehicles. Day trading, swing trading, options trading, fundamental analysis, growth stock investing, value investing, technical analysis, dollar cost averaging and futures trading are all (more or less, anyway) investing styles or approaches.

This leads to an important tenet of active investing: It is a *blended* style. The blended investing style advocated in this book implies a diversification of investing strategies (not just investments themselves) rather than reliance on a single investing vehicle or style. Active investing is not a singular vehicle or style, and it is most emphatically not a panacea. To demonstrate this point, let's examine what happened to some of the recent panaceas, and why investors can no longer follow these clichés directly to the bank.

Buy and Hold

Time was when a simple buy-and-hold approach worked most, if not all, of the time. Warren Buffett did it (and still does), and many financial advisors are quick to point out the average 10 to 11 percent returns from stocks over the past eighty years, if you just hang on. Buy and hold is still a good principle, but it implies that one should just stuff their stock certificates in a safe deposit box or a mattress. Today, this strategy falls victim to shortening business cycles and sometimes to questionable management and financial integrity.

Day Trading

It was a curious and compelling craze. Direct access to markets and instantaneous transactions, all to pick up a few crumbs by buying, selling, buying, and selling. Over and over—ten, twenty, maybe hundreds of times a day. Quit your job, Make a few trades and head to the golf course. Trouble is, the early movers really did have an advantage. Day traders would get in front of the crowd and insert themselves among the real dealers to pick up a small part of the day's gains. Soon, though, there were too many day traders. The real dealers and professionals got smart, and decimal trading cut into the opportunity to earn markup. Today a swift move nets a penny per share, while before 2000 the minimum price increment was one eighth, or 12½ cents per share. Although some trading techniques—and an understanding of the inner workings of the markets—are valuable to today's active investor, day trading as a pure strategy isn't recommended. Among other things, it takes 100 percent (or more) of your focus and time. Active *investors* generally don't have the time and energy.

Traditional Value Investing

As everything washed out in 2001–2002, many grabbed onto the seemingly solid rock of value investing. People looked at business fundamentals again—profits, cash flow, asset valuation, and more eclectic ideas like market dominance and management quality. It was a positive trend. Why? Because rationale is the principal tenet of value investing. The notion that buying shares is like buying a business gets investors much closer to the type of thinking needed to produce sustained return on investments and, as a result, enhance their personal worth. But accounting scandals and the continued difficulty in making any real and timely sense of financial statements continued to get in the way. Also, business changes rapidly. What protects a business today or gives it a competitive edge may change quickly. Finally, the definition of value has been stretched—rightly so—to capture future value in the form of growth, which is theoretically correct but hard to ascertain in practice. Nevertheless, value-investing principles survive to form a key cornerstone of the active investing approach, but active investors are not *just* value investors.

Asset Allocation

The asset allocation rationale is valid, for nobody wants all of their assets tied up in one thing. However, the way it is deployed and marketed to the investing public leaves much to be desired. Brokerage firms proudly announce target asset allocations such as, "55 percent stocks, 35 percent bonds, 10 percent cash." These formulas grab headlines, and, at the grassroots level, send everyone scurrying to their advisors to get the latest pie charts, an analysis of the difference between their positions and the ideal, and—of course—recommendations to bring their portfolio back into alignment. While theoretically sound, asset allocation starts to lose traction when applied to individual investments and portfolios. First of all, the asset class is not as important as the individual asset. Sixty percent stocks is all wrong if an investor owns the wrong stocks. Secondly, the difference between a 60-30-10 percent balance and a 55-35-10 percent balance is trivial for most investors; we're talking about a $2,500 shift for an investor with $50,000 invested. It's hard to see how such an adjustment is the secret to investing success.

True, the approach has merit for very large portfolios like pension and mutual funds, where a few percentage points make a big difference. Making individual shifts toward more conservative investments as one needs to fund a college education or retirement is also sound. But don't belabor us with trivial changes along the way!

A final drawback to asset allocation is its reliance on traditional bonds to build a safer income-based portfolio component. While this is an excellent idea if equity values and interest rates are low (as in 2000), today, considering the prospect of rising interest rates and increased credit risk due to more volatile business conditions, bonds are riskier than ever. Asset allocation models should consider personal assets—like a home—in the mix. In today's environment, paying down a home mortgage can be a better strategy. It's as effective as buying a bond at an equivalent interest rate without the default or the interest rate risk. At one time the prevailing argument against this idea was liquidity; once money was paid into the mortgage it couldn't be retrieved, but today's home equity credit lines address that issue. Could it be that brokers and financial advisors don't advocate this approach because it takes your assets out of their custody?

Diversification

Closely related to asset allocation is the "diversification" mantra. Books and professional advisors all insist on it, and it is both theoretically and practically valid. But it doesn't make sense to diversify to the extent of many recommendations. If you buy two or three large cap mutual funds, you own little overlapped pieces of many companies and you might as well buy an index fund. Overdiversifying, by definition, leads to average market performance; the more diversified you are, the less likely, statistically speaking, you'll be to beat the market.

Dollar Cost Averaging

Dollar cost averaging has been a favorite, particularly of financial journalists, for years. The idea of investing fixed amounts each month is compelling, for (1) it forces a regular savings, which is always a good thing, and (2) the weighted averaging notion implicit in buying more shares of whatever company when prices are low is compelling. It is still important—even with dollar cost averaging—to be aware of what you're investing in, and what it costs to be in that investment. While not a fully active approach, dollar cost averaging has some merit for parts of an active portfolio.

It's About Time

As we make our way through the middle years of the first decade of the new millennium, the swirling waters just explored create a context where savvy investors need to be more diligent than ever to know what they are investing in. Today's investor

. . . can't guess any more, and can't afford to get caught up in investing panaceas.

. . . needs to be mindful of making the most of his or her investments, defending against underperformance while trying to eke out a little more return.

. . . is likely not to be a full-time investor, but instead to have other primary life activities.

. . . accepts the fact that achieving better-than-average returns doesn't come free but requires good research and rationale—not guesswork—to mitigate risk.

. . . looks to diversify not only investments but also investing approaches, time horizons, and risk profiles to achieve improved returns.

As you can imagine, the active investing imperative of today is complex. Defining and developing the active investing style necessary to meet this challenge will be the subject of the rest of this book.

Chapter 3

What Is Active Investing?

The "active investing imperative" developed in the previous chapter arises from more rapidly changing business conditions and increased personal stewardship required to achieve financial goals. The imperative requires you to stay on top of your investments and the external business and political conditions that drive them, and not blindly trust others to do it for you. As an independent investor, you think rationally and strategically, avoiding singular approaches to managing your money. Creativity and *versatility* are increasingly important in today's complex investing world.

Time Is of the Essence

Perhaps most importantly, competent, self-directed investing must be accomplished in a specific context. You are busy with many demands on your time, and investing usually isn't at the top of the list. You are not a professional investor. Whether driven by need or preference, you have other things to do. You have other responsibilities and priorities during the course of a day. You may have an hour a day to deal with your investments, maybe ten or fifteen minutes here or there to check in and get a quote or two, and maybe a couple of hours late in the evening or on a weekend to sit down, digest the week's events, watch a financial network program or two, and do a little research. You are busy and preoccupied with other things. You don't have time to read many investing books, let alone construct detailed financial analyses or charts. You may be able to closely watch a short-term investment, but there will be interruptions and periods of time where you are simply out of pocket or busy dealing with something else. You don't want to lose too much precious mental energy and stress to your investments and especially to the demands of minute-to-minute trading. Bottom line— you'd love to throw it all over the wall to someone else, but you feel compelled not only to stay involved, but also to apply your own touch to the outcome. You're a good candidate to be an active investor.

This chapter defines active investing and identifies its principal tenets that will be covered throughout this book.

A Definition

Several key words regarding active investing have already emerged, including *stewardship, do-it-yourself, blended, versatile, rationale-driven, aware, involved,* and *mildly skeptical*. There are others, including *enlightened* and *strategic*, that will come forward. It's time to stop for the following definition:

> *An active investor manages some or all of his or her portfolio directly and actively, that is with frequent review and response to changing conditions, all with a researched and*

well-constructed rationale for their actions. Active investors do not settle for any single investment style or vehicle. Instead, they employ a blended investing strategy involving combinations of investing vehicles and styles, incorporating short-term and long-term growth and income, and offensive and defensive strategies with varying degrees of professional intermediation. The active investor has other things to do and is not primarily engaged in his or her investing activities.

While this definition helps clarify of active investing, many subtleties and finer points are involved. The rest of this chapter highlights the major principles and tenets of active investing. In the rest of the book, we'll explore pieces of the blended strategy and how they work together to achieve success.

Active Investing Objectives

The major goals of the active investor are:

Asset preservation

The active investor seeks to protect his or her investments from market declines. This is chiefly done by following business cycles, markets, and companies closely and using a value orientation to provide a safety net against large declines. Diversification of investing portfolios and strategies also helps. Some hedging tools, like options, may be employed at times to harvest cash returns from steady or declining investments. In this way (as will be explained later), active investing becomes a moderately *conservative* investing approach.

Above-average asset growth

The active investor seeks to achieve *modestly* better-than-market returns on investments. Achieving financial independence, particularly toward retirement, requires investment performance beyond the core economic growth rate. However, the active investor recognizes the risks in trying to achieve returns *far* in excess of market standards; hence, he or she sets a more realistic "bar" of 1 to 2 percent above the market. Active investors use some relatively low-risk ways to boost return. They use these tools with prudence and due diligence, for they know nothing is free and guesswork doesn't work.

Modest involvement

The active investor is otherwise occupied and simply can't spend all day in front of a computer screen tracking investments, following charts, and reacting to up-to-the-minute news. Active investors work their investment practice around other things and may spend only a few minutes a day on their investments while allocating short periods of "down time" late in the evening or on weekends keeping up. Not only does the active investor not have the time but they also want to avoid the stress and preoccupation associated with full-time real-time investing approaches. To reiterate, active investing isn't day trading.

Core Principles

The active investing approach is multifaceted and somewhat outside the box compared to traditional investing approaches. It is important to understand some of the core principles and tenets.

What Is Active Investing?

Super-diversification

The concept of diversification as ingrained into today's investment world reduces risk by owning multiple asset classes (asset allocation) and multiple investments within a class (as in stocks from a variety of industries). The active investing approach carries this concept further into diversifying one's investing *approaches* or *styles*. What does that mean? That means combining the best of short- and long-term investing; value, growth and income investing; short-term swing trading; options trading; and managed investments strategically into a higher performance portfolio. It also implies a mix of professionally managed and do-it-yourself investments for those with enough to do already. Versatility—the ability to invest flexibly according to market conditions and personal needs—is the key.

Figure 3.1: Active Portfolio Segmentation

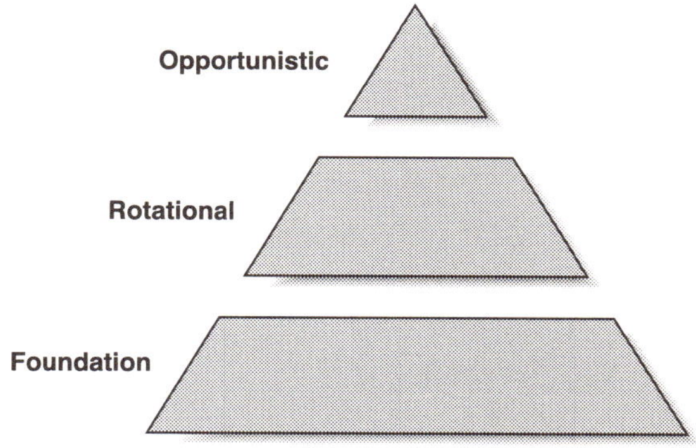

	Classic	Conservative	Aggressive
Opportunistic	10-20%	0-5%	20-40%
Rotational	10-30%	5-20%	10-30%
Foundation	50-80%	80-90%	30-70%

Portfolio Segmentation

Most investors have observed the need to have a few conservative, long-term, income-producing investments mixed in with more aggressive growth investments. The active investing approach suggests a more deliberate, strategic division of your investment portfolio into *foundation, rotational,* and *opportunistic* components or segments. See **Figure 3.1** on page 35.

The Foundation Portfolio

In this construct, each active investor defines and manages a cornerstone *foundation* portfolio. The foundation portfolio is long-term in nature and requires relatively less active management. It frequently consists of retirement accounts (the paradigmatic long-term investment) and may also include your personal residence or other long-lived personal or family assets, such as trusts, collectibles, and so forth (but *not* cars!).

The typical foundation portfolio is invested to achieve at least average market returns through index funds, quality mutual funds, and some income-producing assets (particularly bonds held to maturity or convertible bonds). A foundation portfolio may contain some long-term plays in commodities or real estate to defend against inflation, particularly in such commodities as energy, precious metals, and real estate trusts. The foundation portfolio is largely left alone, although (as with all investments) it is important to check at least once in a while to make sure performance—and anyone being entrusted to manage it—is keeping up with expectations.

The Rotational Portfolio

The second segment is known as the *rotational* portfolio. This segment is managed fairly actively to keep up with changes in business cycles and conditions. A rotational portfolio is a set of stocks or funds that might be rotated or remixed occasionally to reflect business conditions, and to take a more offensive or defensive approach as the market warrants. More than the other portfolios, this portfolio follows the rotation of market preference among different kinds of businesses and business assets. The portfolio is managed to redeploy assets among market or business sectors, between aggressive and defensive business assets, from "large cap" to "small cap" companies; companies with large or small international exposure; companies in favor versus out of favor, from stocks to bonds to commodities, and so forth. Sector-specific exchange-traded funds are a favorite component of these portfolios, as are cyclical and commodity-based stocks like gold mining stocks.

Are we talking about "market timing" when we talk about rotational portfolios? Let's call it "intelligent" or "educated" market timing. Studies telling us that it is impossible to effectively time market moves have been around for years. It is impossible to catch highs and lows in particular investments, market sectors, or even the market as a whole. Nobody can find exact tops or bottoms. But by watching economic indicators and the pulse of business and the marketplace, long-term market performance can be boosted by well-rationalized and timely sector rotation. The key word is timely. The agile active investor has enough of a finger on the pulse to see the signs and invest accordingly.

While the idea isn't new, the advent of "low-friction" exchange-traded funds and other index portfolios makes it a lot more practical for individual investors. What does "low-friction" mean? They trade like a single stock—one order, one discounted commission. In other words, you don't have to liquidate or acquire a whole basket full of investments on your own to follow a sector. We should note that it's been possible to rotate assets in mutual fund families for years with a single phone call, but most funds in these families are less "pure" plays in their sector, and most families do not cover all sectors.

The Opportunistic Portfolio

The *opportunistic* portfolio is the most actively traded portion of an active investor's total portfolio. The opportunistic portfolio looks for stocks or other investments that seem to be notably under- or overvalued at a particular time. The active investor looks to trade these stocks, usually for periods over a few days to a month, to achieve short-term gains. The opportunistic portfolio also looks to generate short-term income through a risk transfer mechanism known as covered option writing. In covered option writing, a possible but low-probability investment outcome is exchanged for a less profitable but more certain outcome. A fee or "premium" is paid in exchange for transferring the opportunity for more aggressive gain to someone else. You collect this premium. Effectively, you as the owner of a stock, can convert a growth investment into an income investment, paying yourself a dividend for the ownership of the stock by selling an option. Is this risky? Actually, it is less risky than owning the stock without selling an option.

Curiously, the main objective of the short-term, opportunistic portfolio is to generate *income,* or cash. Most traditional investors look at the long-term, more conservative components of a portfolio to generate income through bonds, dividend-paying stocks, and so forth. In our active investing framework, the short-term opportunistic portfolio actually does the "heavy lifting" in terms of generating cash income. An active investor might look to trade those stocks with varying degrees of frequency or to sell some options to generate cash. These "swing" trades usually run from a few days to a month or so, and they may be day trades if things work out particularly well and particularly fast. It should be emphasized again that day trades are not the active investor's goal, nor his or her typical practice.

Are Retirement Accounts Always Part of a Foundation Portfolio?

The long-term objectives and nature of retirement accounts suggest normal inclusion as part of the foundation portfolio. Actually, retirement assets can be deployed as part of either the rotational or opportunistic portfolio. And, in fact, it might make a lot of sense. Why? Because returns generated are tax free, at least until withdrawn. Tax-free returns can compound much faster. Because of the importance of these assets, one should only commit a small portion to an actively managed opportunistic portfolio, but it can be a good way to "juice" the growth of this important asset base.

Building Your Own Pyramid

As you might imagine, there is no rule governing the allocation of assets between the three active investing portfolios. How you split your assets is entirely up to you. Some may want to do equal thirds. A more typical "pyramid" approach breaks investments into a larger foundation portfolio, with a midsized rotational portfolio and a relatively small opportunistic segment.

Smaller portfolios might have an as much as 80 percent in a foundation base with the remaining 20 percent in an opportunistic portfolio; thus, there is not enough left to fund the rotational portfolio. The "shape" of your portfolios depends almost entirely on: (1) your tolerance and preference for risk and (2) the time and resources you have to manage investments. The less risk you can tolerate and the less time you have, the broader the base of the pyramid.

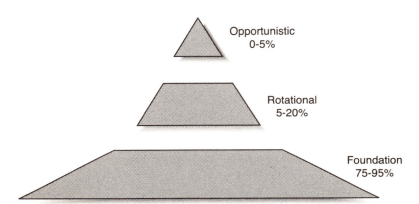

Figure 3.2 Conservative Active Portfolio Segmentation

Opportunistic
0-5%

Rotational
5-20%

Foundation
75-95%

Some investors may not feel compelled—or confident enough—to discern business or market shifts and accordingly manage a rotational portfolio. For this reason, they may stick with the relatively more straightforward foundation and opportunistic portfolios.

Other investors who have more time to actively manage their investments—and the necessary tolerance for risk—may choose to have a larger opportunistic portfolio.

Also worth noting: Portfolio segment size is not set in stone and may be adjusted down the road.

The main point of segmentation is to separate investing objectives and make it easier to apply different strategies, tactics, and investing vehicles to achieve those objectives. Segmentation helps the active investor to stay focused and to track performance. It doesn't matter how large a portfolio is or whether an investor is just starting out—the segmentation approach concept still has merit.

What Is Active Investing? 41

Figure 3.3 Classic Active Portfolio Segmentation

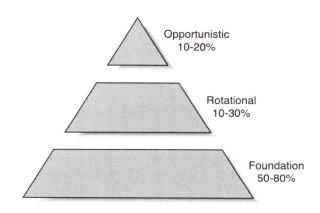

But I Only Have $18,000 to Invest . . .

Such precise division of your investment assets into portfolios may sound a bit over the top for small investors. There may be only a thousand or two in a portfolio. Perhaps all of your invested assets are in retirement plans restricted to company-offered funds. They can't be easily deployed into more active management. There are other problems: Trading small amounts of securities can lead to higher trading costs. Here's the point: Be practical, and don't force-fit your situation to fit the exhibit. It's the thought process that counts—$15,000 in a foundation portfolio (such as a 401(k) plan) and $3,000 in an opportunistic portfolio (such as a Roth IRA) is just fine. Eventually you'll have enough money—and experience—to get the most out of the active approach.

Driven by Rationale

This tenet may seem obvious and straightforward. The active investor has a sound, fundamental business reason for any action taken (or not taken). Such an investor simply does not follow crowds, nor does he or she invest in the latest fad or sexy company. The active investor takes the value investor's approach of investing in a stock as though he or she were buying a business, and these principles apply even if it is intended to be a short-term opportunistic investment. If a stock is undervalued—or overvalued—as a business, it is bought or sold. If an option position is a good risk-reward proposition, it is taken. A sector rotation is done with a similar assessment of events and risks, not only for that investment, but for the entire portfolio. The same goes for the decision to manage a portion of the portfolio individually or by employing an expert. If a certain investment or investment style isn't working out, the active investor assesses the reasons and moves on.

Offense and Defense

The active investor looks to profit from both up and down market moves. While this may attenuate profits available from an "all-up" or "long" position in a rising market, it is the best approach in the long run. Does this tenet indicate the risky approach of selling short? It may, but it doesn't have to. Equity options, index options, and exchange-traded funds afford the opportunity to cash in on downturns with far less risk than by shorting individual stocks.

Organic and Adaptive

Active investing is a *thought process*, not just a set of rules. Rule-based investing, for the most part, doesn't work. There are too many unknowns, and there are sharks in the water waiting for people who abide *en masse* by certain rules. Set a stop loss order at 10 percent below the current price, like all the books tell you to?

There is probably a market maker (a dealer) out there ready to sop up shares at a discount from the unwary. This isn't to condemn such a rule as useless, only to recognize that it's better to think than to follow set rules. Sure, if you've already made 50 percent on a stock and are about to leave on a three-day retreat to central nowhere twenty-five miles from a phone—by all means, enter the protection. Rules can call you out to action or to make a decision, but they shouldn't make the decision for you. While it's important to detach from your investments *emotionally*, rational investing does have some subjective elements. Good investing is art combined with science, and the active thought process takes that into account.

The Active Investor Lives on a Budget

Just as active investors have something else to do with their *time*, they also have something else to do with their *money*. Active investors don't have the wherewithal to spend thousands on expensive research services like Hoover's, Standard & Poor's, and other high end financial information services. They may subscribe to a newsletter or two, but they generally rely on their own judgment, not that of others. Active investors are experts at getting as much information as possible for free using the Internet and other resources—and there's a lot out there. Having said that, there are a few things worth paying money for. The next chapter recommends access to the Value Line Investment Survey, a great summary of important financial data, business performance, and growth prospects for important companies. True, it costs about $600 per year, but it is probably worth it. But before writing that check, stop by the local library—you might just find it there. Bottom line: It doesn't cost thousands of dollars to become an active investor.

The Active Investing Style, Summarized

Here is a summary of the major tenets of active investing:

OBJECTIVE

Enhanced returns, reduced risk
- Modestly beat market returns while maintaining a margin of safety

APPROACHES

Blended strategy
- Mix of styles, tools, approaches
- Versatile, adaptive, offense, and defense
- Segmented portfolio: foundation, rotation, opportunistic
- Do-it-yourself and professional management

Rational approach
- Strong business rationale
- Enlightened by best and most current information available
- Value oriented

Modest involvement
- Aligned to busy lifestyle
- Not a full-time activity
- Inexpensive resources

Is Active Investing for You?

Active investing is all about learning from previous mistakes and taking charge of your investing life. It is about adapting your personal investing practice to the times. It is about logical, rational thought, and it is relatively conservative in goals and approach. It does take some work to do the "due diligence" to monitor markets and the business climate, select investments, track the results, and learn from those events. Like anything else worth doing, it takes time to master the techniques but also to learn the *craft*. It takes some patience, and it may take some outside help or resources. Active investing will take some *personal* investment, but even if you adapt just some of the thought process, you're likely to come out ahead.

What Comes Next

It would be logical to expect the rest of the book to be divided according to the portfolio segments outlined earlier. Chapters would be aligned to explain how to manage the foundation, rotational, and opportunistic portfolios. This book isn't set up that way. Why? Because the fundamental concepts of value investing, short-term trading, exchange traded funds, options, mutual funds, and so forth can apply to all three segments. No matter which portfolio you're working, you need to know fundamental value investing to understand (1) which businesses are good, and (2) whether they are selling at an attractive value. Commodities can appear in any portfolio, as can options. You get the point.

Here is the sequence of what lies ahead:

- Part II: *The Informed and Equipped Active Investor* contains four chapters that cover the information sources and trading tools you need to be familiar with in order to become a successful active investor.
- Part III: *The Quest for Value* provides a practical construct for assessing the financial and strategic value of a business for investments across all portfolios.
- Part IV: *Trading Tools and Techniques for Active Investors* switches gears to opportunistic short-term trading techniques.
- Part V: *Blending Investments and Investing Styles* covers funds, options, and other vehicles that you can use to broaden your investing opportunities. The book's final chapter,

Putting Active Investing into Practice, connects the dots to build your active investing practice and also gives several examples of how you can individualize this approach to your own situation.

Anyone who has read investing books or has attended lectures or seminars has experienced the depth and complexity of the science of investing. This book's approach is more one of breadth than of depth; it's a view of a strategic thought process as much as of a specific technique. Not every technique can be explored in depth, and for those topics you will learn what questions to ask, and what to examine further. For many investors, that's the most important result.

Part II:

The Informed and Equipped Active Investor

Chapter 4

Windows to the Investing World

Let's "take stock" of where we've been so far. In answer to today's complex and rapidly changing business environment, the first part of this book made the case for the *active* investing approach—an *independent, strategic,* and *enlightened* approach to growing wealth. The point is to grow invested assets at rates at or slightly above market returns and the economy as a whole, all achieved in the limited time and resource context of having another profession or something else to do.

Not surprisingly, the "enlightened" part of this equation starts with *information.* The title of this chapter, "Windows to the Investing World," describes the set of resources through which active investors become and stay enlightened. In Chapter 6, we will explore the set of resources through which these investors actually invest (i.e., investing platforms), such as the brokerage and trading services that give access to the securities markets. In active investing, enlightenment is more important than execution; that is, more effort should be placed toward acquiring knowledge and making good investing decisions. The choice of brokers or trading platforms is relatively straightforward and "commoditized," as there is little differentiating the services. Put another way, a good investing strategy with a lousy investing platform is easier to fix than a bad or poorly informed investing strategy with a good trading platform.

It All Starts with Information

The active investor, to perform his or her craft, must stay attuned to today's business and investment climate. Active investors must tune into information at many levels in order to make sense of the global economy and events that affect business, understand business at an industry level, and follow specific companies or businesses as investments.

Objective: Figure Out Where the Puck Is Going

The spectrum of information the active investor strives to capture ranges from very high-level economic indicators such as interest rates, unemployment, and trade balances, to specific company data such as earnings, cash flow, balance sheet, and marketplace performance. The active investor must figure out how indicators such as economic and industry performance *apply* to their businesses, and then understand the businesses themselves as investments.

Boiled down, the active investor uses news and information as part of a discovery process to track change and to identify opportunities. It's a fact of business life that every industry has its leaders and laggards. Investing is—as much as anything else—not about figuring out where businesses have been but rather where they are going. As such, the enlightened investor compiles all indicators to assess who will be the *future* leaders and laggards. The active investor examines the *calculus* of business and his/her investments—that is, change, direction of change, and size of change, not just where things have been or where they are today. Hockey great Wayne Gretzky became great by developing an extraordinary sense of where the puck was going, and that lesson should never be lost on the active investor.

All Sizes and Shapes

The democratization of investing described in Chapters 1 and 2 has come about largely from the broader real-time availability of more information to more people through the Internet. As little as ten years ago the average investor—and many more sophisticated investors—had few information sources beyond the morning newspaper and a few periodicals.

Monthly Is Not Enough

"Daily and weekly" media? What about monthly? Much of what is published on a monthly basis is just a little too dated to be relevant. Considering editorial deadlines, some of the information might be as much as two months old in a "current" issue. While commentary in such publications as *Money* and *Smartmoney* magazines might contribute to an overall understanding of the business and investing environment, be careful with their investment recommendations. The long lead time on articles may mean their recommendations are behind the curve. Online versions might prove better, but beware of the long load times found on a traditional modem connection and excessive advertising.

So what does the Internet add? Try: (1) real-time, (2) deeper, and (3) more customizable information. Through the Internet, active investors can track news events as they happen; this enables them to (as the cliché goes) "level the playing field" with other investors. But the Internet also uncovers deeper information about industries and individual companies—news releases, financial information, and editorial analysis and commentary from the financial press. You can examine the data, draw charts, screen the data, and perform analysis according to your own special set of criteria. "Information is power" is another cliché, but it really describes what is going on today: more access to information used quickly and productively to become more enlightened and to make better decisions.

Today's investing information comes in all sizes and shapes. The active investor should employ a small and diverse smorgasbord of information sources including traditional daily and weekly print and selected online media. The exact mix chosen will depend on personal preference and the amount of time you choose to dedicate to discovery.

A Preferred Set of Information Resources

An Internet search on "investing" will bring up an overwhelming number of resources available to the average investor. Add to that the shelves of business and investing periodicals and books and it's easy to see how information acquisition could quickly get out of hand. There simply isn't enough time in a day (or a week or month, for that matter) to digest it all. Not to mention the cost. While most Internet resources are free, some do cost money, as do most print resources. It is possible to spend thousands of dollars a year on a single information source. The active-investing context recognizes your limited time and resources. You have a few minutes a day, a few hours here and there on an evening or weekend, and a limited budget to spend on information.

While active investing is not full-time investing, the active investor keeps a finger on the pulse of daily economic and business events. The "daily" list requires the most adept balancing between "enough" and "too much." It is easy to become overwhelmed by seeing the same things over and over. The goal is to become enlightened without becoming burned out. What this means in practice varies among investors. Those preferring a more active style or dealing in more volatile investments, such as technology stocks or commodity futures, will necessarily have to invest more in daily reconnaissance. Those dealing with more conservative trades or smaller "opportunistic" portfolios will spend less time engaged. That being said, every active investor should follow some daily news. Here is a daily "musts" and "nice-to-haves" list.

Must: A Financially Oriented Daily Newspaper

A financially oriented newspaper is one that carries detailed business news and investment performance. Every active investor should get—or have access to—at least one. *The Wall Street Journal* is best for a balanced look at macroeconomic, marketplace, and detailed investing information, organized conveniently by section. A *Journal* read, if sometimes a bit dry, is a balanced update. *Investor's Business Daily* slants more toward technical investing information. *The New York Times* has less investing news but more coverage of financial industry and regulatory trends. *USA Today* gives broad, though not very detailed, coverage.

Must: A Financial Portal

Financial portals provide real-time or delayed stock quotes plus an assortment of other investing information either directly on the site or through links to other sites. Among the many options, Yahoo!Finance is the best *(finance.yahoo.com)*. Yahoo!Finance supplies delayed quotes, some real-time market data, up-to-the-minute news summaries from an assortment of wire services, and a strong assortment of resources to evaluate individual stocks and specialized investments, including mutual and exchange-traded funds. Additional "fee" reports can be purchased usually for a modest $5 to $10. You'll also find economic and earnings calendars. A fifteen-minute-a-day Yahoo!Finance tour is an effective and efficient way to track macro and micro events. Valuable pages include:

- The *"Finance Home"* main page summarizes market action and gives access to quotes, charts, and links to other important parts of the site *(finance.yahoo.com)*.
- The *"Market Overview"* page gives deeper analysis of the day's market activity, plus links into "In Play," Upgrades/Downgrades, and other individual company detail *(finance.yahoo.com/mo)*.
- *"In Play,"* sourced from Briefing.com, is a near-real-time summary and analysis of market conditions and individual "story stocks" *(finance.yahoo.com/mp)*.
- *Exchange Traded Funds (ETF) Center* is a sub-portal specializing in ETFs and overall sector performance. As will be explained later, ETFs are an important tool in the active investor's toolbox and aren't as well covered (yet) as individual stocks in the financial media. So this center is a valuable resource. A subpage listing more than 120 ETFs sorted by daily performance shows which sectors are hot and which are not. *(finance.yahoo.com/etf, finance.yahoo.com/etf/browser/mkt)*
- *Company analysis.* Enter a stock symbol and a whole menu of analytical tools opens up to understand the company, including company profile, financial summaries and details, news, analyst coverage, and charts for that company. Nearly all traded companies are covered, and almost everything is fast and free (go to *finance.yahoo.com*, enter a ticker symbol for a quote).

Windows to the Investing World

There are other portals, like CNNfn, Bloomberg, and CNBC, they are harder to use, not as broad and complete, and more burdened with advertising.

Cost: usually zero.

Near-Must: Briefing.com

Briefing.com is a real-time broadcast of breaking business news and commentary. Briefing is more than a portal, it adds in its own concise analysis and real-time access to broker upgrades and downgrades and individual analyst comments on "story" stocks. Briefing provides detailed earnings and economic calendar information. The basic Briefing service is free; "gold" and "platinum" services offer more real-time commentary. Live alerts, called "In Play," help to keep investors abreast of the latest developments with an individual stock. A subscription to Briefing.com "gold" and "platinum" services is especially attractive for the more active investor. Yahoo!Finance offers many pieces of the Briefing.com service.

Cost: zero, $9.95/mo. for Gold, $24.95/mo. for the Platinum service (*www.briefing.com*).

Nice-to-Have: CNBC

Those who do have the time and access to cable or satellite TV are well served by tuning in occasionally to CNBC. CNBC has the well-known ticker "crawler" across the bottom with real-time quotes. Naturally you can track the daily progress of the markets. The "Morning Call" and the more acerbic "Kudlow & Cramer" segments offer good commentary. But it is easy to reach saturation watching too much of this channel. CNBC is especially useful when markets become volatile or when you have very short-term "plays" on the table.

Cost: Cable TV service and time spent watching repeated dull ads.

Nice-to-Have: *Nightly Business Report*

PBS puts out this very well-designed half-hour show each evening in most of its markets, usually around dinnertime each weekday. Each show examines the day's economic events and market activity with focus on the biggest movers of the day, interesting guest commentary, and industry reviews.

Cost: nothing; except an implied duty to support your local PBS station. *Marketplace* from National Public Radio (NPR), hosted by David Brown, plays a similar role but with less detail.

Nice-to-Have: E-mail Newsletters

Again, you can go nuts sorting through the cacophony of newsletters and investment advisories; it is advisable to stick with a very limited handful or none at all. There are many, many trading newsletters with today's "best ideas." For the most part they should be avoided, as they are more about hype than good fundamental advice. If you have a newsletter that you like and trust (for a reasonable price)—and you have time for it—it never hurts to have another window to the market.

Weekly and Other Information Sources

"Daily enlightenment" is only part of the active investor's quest. It is oriented to tracking smaller changes and identifying shorter-term opportunities, although collectively the daily inputs serve to build a more complete and enduring picture of what's going on. A small assortment of additional resources are recommended to round out the information toolbox and provide the more in-depth analysis of specific businesses and industries.

Must: One Weekly Business Newsmagazine

While you can sense what's going on by absorbing the daily bubblings of the financial world, it's helpful to step back into a concise summary of the week's events and get a big-picture view of certain businesses and industries. *BusinessWeek* summarizes change in the economic and investing environment with detailed journalistic examination of specific companies and businesses. *The Economist*, based in Great Britain, adds a stronger world slant and a more contrarian view of most business and economic factors. Getting both publications is seldom redundant. The cost is $60/year for *BusinessWeek* and about $100/year for *The Economist*.

Near-Must: Value Line

If you subscribe to the viewpoint that buying a stock is like buying a business (and that viewpoint will be developed later on in Chapter 8), then, as a rationale-driven active investor, you need a source of information to appraise that business. With that in mind, among the many investment resources available, Value Line is one of the select few worth a financial commitment.

A mixed print and Internet resource, the Value Line Investment Survey offers concise business and financial summaries across a universe of 1,700 companies. Weekly updates cover companies in five or six chosen sectors and give an overview of activity in that sector. Each company is reviewed approximately four times a year. Review pages summarize the company's business and market position and recent developments, along with key financial information and stock price performance. Value Line adds "Timeliness" and "Safety" ratings. The Timeliness rating, while not foolproof, is a good indicator for active investors looking for rotational and other short-term opportunities. As the name indicates, Value Line emphasizes a value-oriented investing approach.

Daily Information Sources Compared

Active Investing Daily Information Resources

Resource	Type	Description	Advantages	Disadvantages	Cost
Wall Street Journal	Daily business paper	Complete economic, marketplace, financial news	Strong marketplace info	Cost	$350/yr
Investor's Business Daily	Daily investing paper	Daily investing summary and detail	In-depth investing and trading news	Not as rounded as WSJ, little on marketplace	$295/yr
New York Times	National daily paper	Complete paper with Business and World Business sections	Summarizes political and economic climate, regulatory activities	Cost	$49.50/mo
USA Today	National daily paper	Complete daily with "Money" section	Good business and investing overview	Broad but not deep	$125/yr
City daily papers		Local and national news, business summary and major stock quotes	Inexpensive broad coverage and interest	Not in-depth, many have incomplete financial and investment data	$10–$40/mo

Windows to the Investing World

Yahoo!Finance	Internet Portal	Quotes, news, company financials, investing and personal finance information	Broad coverage, easy to use, usually free	Information, but not much insight	Free
Briefing.com	Financial news portal	Latest economic and business news releases, analysis	Excellent portrayal of analysis of economic data, value-add company news releases and analysis in near real-time	Too time-consuming for some investors	Free $9.95/mo Gold $29.95/mo Platinum
CNBC	National cable/satellite financial news network	Real-time quotes plus full time market analysis and commentary	Up-to-the-minute news, quotes	Can be time-consuming	Free
Nightly Business Report	PBS show	Daily half-hour financial news summary	Good overview of day's market and economic activity	Not much detail	Free
Newsletters	Daily e-mail updates	Up-to-the-minute financial and economic commentary, trading tips	Provides additional viewpoints, trading ideas	Many are poor-quality, biased, or take too much time	Some free, some fee

In addition to the flagship 1,700-stock Value Line Investment Survey, Value Line offers several specialized investment products of interest to active investors, among them a Small and Mid-Cap Edition, a Mutual Fund Survey, an Exchange-Traded-Funds (ETF) Survey, and a "Special Situations" survey, which puts a weekly spotlight on a handful of very high potential stocks. While Value Line has an excellent performance track record and puts good information and "value add" analysis into a few pages, cost is the chief downside. The basic Investment Survey is $598 per year (with an attractive 13-week trial offer at $75), The other resources generally run between $50 and $300 per year. Value Line offers an attractive seven-publication "Value Line Research Center" bundle for $1,790 per year. The basic Investment Survey at $598 may be worth it for the typical active investor for no other reason than it saves a lot of research time. But before writing that check, know that the basic Value Line Investment Survey is often found at the local public library. Value Line resources are described and offered at *www.valueline.com*.

Near-Must: Morningstar

What Value Line is to individual stocks, Morningstar has been for years to mutual funds and other fund investments. Morningstar carved its niche in ranking and rating the expansive universe of mutual funds, classifying them by investing style, tracking performance, and providing key statistics on fees and costs.

While this is where Morningstar excels, their coverage has expanded into exchange-traded funds (ETFs—more on them in Chapter 13) and has moved into tracking and analyzing individual companies. Individual company analysis isn't as deep or rigorous as that offered by Value Line, and has a more conservative bias, but it is still a useful read and can help as a second opinion. One unique feature: Morningstar individual stock ratings

Windows to the Investing World 61

describe the size of strength of each company's "moat"—a Buffettonian metaphor for barriers to competition.

Figure 4.1: Morningstar snapshot

The "good" parts of Morningstar also require a subscription fee, but the modest $12.95 a month is reasonable. Active investors with an orientation toward mutual funds or ETFs are well advised to take this subscription, and, as mentioned, it also provides some alternative analysis for individual stocks. Predictably, the site is *www.morningstar.com*.

Morningstar "Amazon"

Morningstar recently launched a feature taken straight out of the pages of online bookseller Amazon.com. Just as Amazon lists the books that readers of a chosen book also bought, Morningstar now provides a popup message when a user examines a report on a specific fund. "Investors who viewed this fund also viewed . . ." goes the tagline. Although this is probably a useful feature when sifting through the 9,200 funds in the mutual fund universe, for some it may feel too much like shopping for a simple retail product.

Nice-to-Have: The Motley Fool

"Educate, Amuse, and Enrich" are the stated themes and goals of The Motley Fool, a fully loaded investing Web site and service aimed mainly at knowledgeable do-it-yourself investors. "The Fool" gives straightforward, refreshing and slightly contrarian view of the markets, investing strategy and individual investments. Story stocks are followed closely. A staff of analysts adds timely, high-quality commentary. Analyst reports share the rationale and technique behind their comments, thus making The Fool a good way to learn, as well as to stay informed. Most services are free in return for a registration and a fairly heavy load of advertising and promotion *(www.fool.com)*.

Nice-to-Have: *Business 2.0* or Similar

It is always good to have a nonfinancial view of business, especially where the focus is on new business and business change.

Windows to the Investing World

Business 2.0 is probably the best of a handful of magazines born during the late 1990s boom at tracking new companies, new things at old companies, and new ways of doing business in general. Remember, as mentioned in Chapter 1, the imperative to keep track of how new technologies and ideas are adopted by older businesses. The content of these magazines, while at times a little "way out," give a look at where the puck is going for certain business segments, and are a bargain at (usually) less than $20 per year.

Does It Make Sense to Pay for Research Reports?

Before making any source of information part of your repertoire, you must assess whether the value derived from it is proportionate to the time and money invested in it. As you develop your active style, you'll find some things more enlightening than others, more efficient to read and more tailored to your specific style and interests. Every active investor tries out several sources before settling on a personal best assortment. But the $64 question—and it often costs more than that—is "Is it worth paying for research reports?" It's clearly a matter of personal preference—and return on investment. The resourceful active investor finds ways to get most of "the good stuff" for free—Value Line at the library, Briefing.com through Yahoo!Finance and through the Briefing Web site, Standard & Poor's reports through a personal broker, and so forth. Does paying for another report make you a better investor? Sometimes convenience and timeliness override cost. Again, like investing itself, think "return on investment."

Chapter 5

Through the Window: What Active Investors Look For

Now, with this information in hand, the obvious question is—what do active investors *do* with it all? What do active investors look for through these windows? In a nutshell, active investors are looking for "macro" and "micro" information. Macro information concerns the economy, business cycle, industries, and the markets. Micro information refers to information about the financial, marketplace, and investment performance of individual companies and their stocks. All investors—and particularly the more active variety—are well served to keep track of economic events and the business cycle. These ideas are further developed in Chapter 7.

The Business Cycle

Through a series of indicators and changes in those indicators, active investors track the changes in business conditions. Is the economy in an expansion phase? A contraction phase? A transition phase? Different industries—and thus, different businesses—will prosper depending on these conditions. Through a series of economic indicators, investors can get a good idea of where the business cycle—and where the markets—are going. Active investors are also watching for "secular" trends—that is, business sectors that are moving contrary to the overall business cycle, as energy or retailers did through much of the 2001–2003 recession.

Interest Rates

Few factors influence markets in the short and long term as much as interest rates. Interest rates have the combined effect of stimulating or retarding business activity and making various investments more or less attractive. Active investors monitor interest rates at all levels—the "Fed," bond and mortgage interest rates, not only for where they are but where they are going and why. In recent years, for instance, the Fed "bias" has become just as important as actual interest rates or current interest rate changes.

Inflation

The other "I" word in investing, inflation, and its effects, are critical. Investors watch for real and perceived changes in inflation. In recent years, inflation has caused divergent effects on different businesses and business sectors. Whether or not inflation is good for a business is determined to a great extent by whether or not a business is able to pass on cost increases—in other words, do they have pricing power? Pricing power, discussed more in Chapter 9, is a strong company differentiator. The disparity has grown in recent years between businesses that can pass on cost increases—healthcare, energy, utilities—and those that cannot—airlines, information technology, autos, durable goods, and many consumer products. Indicated changes in consumer and producer, or wholesale, prices should be tracked. Not only does inflation intrinsically affect business, but it also leads to changes in interest rates through Fed policy.

International Trade

In today's global economy, trade and its cause-and-effect relationships with the strength or weakness of the U.S. dollar have become ever more important to watch. Certain businesses—those with large international markets or important international sources of supply—will naturally be more affected by trade in general and the level of the dollar in particular. Expanding trade deficits can foretell higher interest rates (to cool import demand and strengthen the dollar), and trade policy in economically sensitive industries like steel and semiconductors also must be followed by investors in those industries.

Productivity

Much of the economic progress in the last twenty years of the twentieth century has arisen from productivity increases. Productivity increases are the economic crown jewel of the technology boom (like it or not, just consider how much more work you can do in a day with things like e-mail, voice mail, and PCs). Productivity leads to "free" economic expansion—that is, more output without a corresponding increase in input. When productivity increases start to slow, that foretells poorer return on investment in the economy and certain industries. This leads to inflation, as more pressure is put on inputs and input prices in order to sustain a level of output. The effects of productivity on specific investments is less direct than with many other macro factors, but it bears watching as a leading indicator of other economic events.

Sentiment Indicators

Consumer confidence and manufacturing sentiment indicators can lead to strong short-term changes in market bias and activity in specific sectors. The Conference Board Consumer Confidence Survey and the University of Michigan Consumer

Sentiment Index are key indicators on the consumer side; the National Association of Purchasing Managers and the Chicago PMI (Purchasing Managers Index) are good short-term leading indicators of business activity. Employment reports not only convey real information about the state of the economy, but are also more and more a sentiment indicator, as hiring plans directly reflect the aggregate "take" of corporate managers on the short- and long-term economic future. Taking the employment report apart into component sectors (e.g., manufacturing, retail, construction) can be even more revealing.

Industry Indicators

Active investors watch different sectors of the economy; it is rather like shopping for products by first examining the store. There are a number of ways to do this, although none are truly ideal. Graphic representations of sector performance and of individual companies in those sectors are available in each Monday's edition of *USA Today* (at the back of the Money section) and at smartmoney.com *(www.smartmoney.com/marketmap)*. The customization features in the smartmoney.com mapping section are useful as they can be set to reflect the timeframes you want (1 day, 1 week, 26 weeks, 52 weeks, etc.). You can also examine subsectors—that is, the component sectors of the Technology sector, like semiconductors, software, computer hardware, and telecommunications equipment.

Finally, it is easy to determine which individual companies lead and lag sector performance, and how much influence that company has on the sector. The downside of smartmoney.com is download time; it is complex and a bit slow on traditional modem connections.

One can also get a flavor for strong and weak sectors by following the Exchange Traded Funds (ETFs) tracking those sectors. The Yahoo!Finance ETF Browser (within the "ETF Center"; hit "view all" ETFs) gives a quick look at daily, three-month, and year-to-date sector performance. Finally, active investors choosing to specialize in certain sectors or subsectors will want to follow published media in those sectors: industry and trade publications, newsletters, Web sites, and so forth. This is particularly easy to do if they work in that industry, as the publications and industry "scoop" is readily available. If it's there, take advantage of it!

Expanding Your Sector IQ

Sector familiarity and investing has really come into its own for individual investors fairly recently. In part this is because of the greater tendency in recent years for certain sectors to outperform others. In part it is due to the growth in practical means—sector-specific mutual funds and ETFs—for investing in sectors. Dow Jones—creator of the segment structure used by Smartmoney.com and a purveyor of many sector investing products, offers a good section on sector investing on the "InvestIQ" section of their Web site. Check out: *http://dowjones.investiq.com/dowjones/isec_rotation.html* for more details.

The Detailed View

Obviously, the real money to be made in active investing comes from specific investments in specific companies or funds. The macro view just discussed provides enlightenment regarding overall economic and business conditions and trends; it should be followed consistently, if not on a daily basis. The rubber meets the road, however, in the micro exercise of choosing and tracking individual investments. Here is a condensed version of the "micro" view.

Company Performance

First and foremost, active investing is *rational* investing, and an active investor strives to understand as much as possible about a company's current performance, performance history, and projected future performance. Active investors are independent and thus develop their own views. Although they pay attention to a degree to what the outside world and especially professional analysts say, they work hard to develop their own take. Active investors look at financial performance, including balance sheet, income statement, and cash flow data. Yahoo!Finance and its links to Multex financial pages provide the easiest and quickest view. Value Line, however, is probably best. Annual reports have devolved into slick and outdated marketing brochures for most companies, and they are of relatively little use except for providing detail on certain financial items. (To this end, the more complete "10-K" filing required by the Securities and Exchange Commission [SEC] can be an interesting, if laborious, read.) Chapter 9, which covers value investing further, describes the discovery of company performance.

Marketplace Performance

A company must create value in its marketplace before it can create financial value for its investors. The "marketplace" is not the stock market, but rather the business-to-consumer or business-to-business market into which the firm sells its products or services. Most traditional or "fundamental" investors focus too much on financials, which effectively represent where the puck has been, and not enough on marketplace factors, which dictate where the puck is going. One reason: Marketplace factors are much harder to assess. Market share and customer preference statistics aren't published on a regular basis. The active investor makes his/her own assessment through an assortment of market-oriented published business material like the *Wall Street Journal* and *BusinessWeek*. This judgment should be supplemented where possible by an "on-the-ground" assessment of the success of a business in its marketplace. Investment guru and former fund manager Peter Lynch once suggested investing in businesses apparently doing well on the street, with good products and happy customers as a good place to start. Savvy investors look at new products and product announcements and new strategic initiatives brought to market, many of which are covered by the various news wire services.

Management Performance

It is tough to assess the quality of a firm's management (unless it's under the journalistic spotlight for some specific and usually egregious event). Management evaluation is usually done through financial and marketplace performance, although key signals can be taken from the frequency and clarity ("transparency") of communication from the managers involved. As Warren Buffett has said, "Managers that talk about problems are more likely to fix them." Active investors prefer a management team committed to working on their behalf, and they are constantly tuned in to look for signs as to whether or not management is doing so.

Financial Market Performance

The previous two points refers to a company's position as a *business*. Yet you must also consider the company's performance as an *investment*. Active investors track stock prices and price performance, remaining constantly aware that prices may differ from actual business performance. Prudent personal financial management naturally entails keeping track of the price and value of a portfolio—that is, the investments you have already made. Active investors also keep track of the price behavior of prospective investments to determine when an investment is an attractive short- or long-term value. Charts are an important tool for this exercise. The active investor also looks at the market perception of the business—is good news well received and rewarded by the market (as in share price) or is it largely ignored? Finally, the active investor keeps track of specific business events, like earnings releases, not only for the specific companies being followed but also others in the industry.

Chapter 6

Executing Your Strategy: Platforms for Active Investors

So far, Part II of this book has explored ways to stay tuned into the business world and to individual investments. The other point of contact, or "window," to the investing world is through the trading platform used to actually execute your investments.

Investing books habitually make a big deal of comparing brokerage services and dissecting each down to the infinitesimal detail of features and benefits. Recognizing two things—(1) these services are very competitive and change constantly, and (2) overall quality, versatility, and economy are more important than high performance—will make clear what's important at a high level. All that will be left for you to do is to kick the tires and slam the doors on your own.

Aftermath of a Perfect Storm

The 1999–2003 market roller coaster had hardly a more profound effect anywhere than in the brokerage industry. The rapid influx of active, independent, and inexperienced traders mixed with technology breakthroughs like the Internet and direct network access led to an explosion of sexy new trading platforms aimed at the *very* active trader making tens and even hundreds of trades in a day. Those who had the time and stamina (and who could pay up to $20 per trade) used these "high- performance jets" to become real-time players—dealers—in the market. Edgy names like Tradehard.com, Cybertrader, and Pristine Trader became fashionable to drop at parties, and traders quit their jobs or "retired" in droves to take a seat behind the flashing large-format monitors required to make use of it all.

Active Trading, by the Numbers

Market researcher TowerGroup published a study of online trading history and future projection. Average daily online trading volume went from a meager 10,000 trades per day in 1995 to 361,000 per day in 1998 to 800,000 per day in 1999 and just slightly fewer than that in 2000. Then, the crash—down to 511,000 in 2001, and to a low of 390,000 in 2002—a 50 percent decrease. From there, they project an 8 percent compounded increase to 624,000 by the year 2008. Online trading is here to stay and is back on a growth path. Evidently, though, some hard lessons have been learned and the craze is over.

During the late 1990s, most other investors with a PC and few bucks to throw into the ring adopted the more mild-mannered online trading platforms. Existing brokerages like Charles Schwab tinkered with Web-based trading; new Internet-based trading platforms like E-Trade and Datek came on line; and even full-service brokerages reluctantly stuck their toes into the pool. Each broker tinkered and tweaked with their sites—and bombarded consumers with advertising—to try to take the lead. Then as the tide washed out they starting tinkering with price—i.e., commissions—to restart flagging trading volume. As it turned out that just lowered revenues further.

Faced with this conundrum of declining revenues and declining interest, beleaguered online brokers went into a huddle to rethink their business models. The first step was research. They discovered a group of customers who traded actively but were also very demanding in terms of trading performance and service, even though few of these people were actually full-time professional traders.

To satisfy this group, the larger retail online brokerages started to buy the high-performance jets to integrate their best features into their existing offerings. As examples, Schwab bought Cybertrader and Ameritrade bought Datek and its Watcher engine. The result is a convergence of the best features of the high-performance engines, once available only to serious day traders at a fairly high cost, with a basic set of features required by all investors. This bundle was brought to market at prices much more reasonable than those of the exclusive high-performance platforms of the late 1990s. The idea is to capture not only the serious day trader, but the much larger emerging market of more sophisticated active investors—like you.

Today's Landscape: Something for Everyone

As the post-crash era recedes, the consolidation in investing platforms continues. Today, online brokers are offering different levels of service in complete packages, or in some cases, sort of an à-la-carte format. Some customers want more investment advice and are willing to pay for it in higher commissions and even fees. Some want a very active high-performance platform geared to full-time trading. But there is an expanding middle group of savvy and active customers who want some of the benefits of trading tools and reduced commissions, along with *some* (not a lot) of service, research, and analysis. They will trade frequently—maybe two, five, ten, or twenty times a month, but not necessarily daily. They are self-directed, independent, and fairly sophisticated. Who are these middle-ground investors? You guessed it—active investors.

The hottest battleground among consumer brokerages is for this middle and potentially most profitable segment. The catch with most of these services is that, to get the low advertised commissions, you must demonstrate high activity.

But My Broker Offers Services for Active Traders . . .

Most brokers still hang the term "active trader" on the middle-ground investor who isn't a day trader but also isn't a professionally managed account. For the purposes of this book, the active *trader* is focused on trading and probably considers trading daily while actually doing so at least ten times a month. Active traders make their money by involving substantial portions of their portfolios in market action. They are more concerned with capturing price movements and less concerned about the value of the underlying security or business. Active *investors*, on the other hand, build a more complete, segmented portfolio, with certain portions of it remaining quite inactive. Their more moderate goals are limited to producing just a few percentage points better than a market return. They seek to add a modest income to their portfolio through trading. Because brokers primarily make their money from trading activity, they may be truly targeting active traders with their midrange services. But what suits their active *trader* also largely suits the needs of the active *investor*.

That can be expensive—requiring as much as $2,640 a year in extra commissions in the case of Fidelity ($29.95 standard commission less $8 discount commission, times 120 trades). However, you can often talk a representative into a trial period in which you can demonstrate activity at the lower rate. You may also be able to show a prior track record at another firm. It usually takes a minimum net asset value to qualify; this minimum usually ranges from $30,000 to $50,000.

The Active Investing Menu

Choosing a brokerage product requires understanding the features—and mix of features—offered for the cost. Online brokerage services offer so many features as to be confusing to almost anyone; here are some of the more common ones. Obviously, as you develop your active style, your specific needs will evolve accordingly.

"Streaming" and "Real-Time" Quotes and News

Active investors need to keep up with the events of the day and the prices of current and potential investments. Real-time news and quotes are fairly standard among brokerage offerings, and are available through most of the other online portals mentioned earlier in this chapter. Real-time news comes from an assortment of wire services such as Reuters, Business Wire, Associated Press, and Comtex. These stories are captured at a macro level and for each publicly traded company.

The difference between "real-time" and "streaming" is important for some investors. "Real-time" means that you must refresh your screen to get the latest, while "streaming" means that updates occur automatically in your full browser or a condensed browser window on your desktop. Streaming quotes act like a real-time ticker, where the latest trades scroll across your screen. "Watch

Lists"—on-screen trackers of a group of stocks—are nice to have, as are e-mail or telephone alerts when specific prices are met.

Active investors should have some access to real-time quotes. Delayed quotes are good for most situations and general investment tracking, but they will fall short in some close trading situations. Quotes should include not only the last trade but also the "inside" bid and offer, or ask prices (these terms are reviewed in Chapter 10). These "inside" quotes are referred to as "Level I" by NASDAQ and by online brokerage services.

Level II Quotes

Level II quotes are the luxury package upgrade of the financial platform industry. As will be described in Chapter 10, NASDAQ is a dealer, or "market maker" marketplace, where dealers in a particular security come together to place at least one bid and offer on a handled security. The NASDAQ system is little more than an electronic quote board (as the acronym for National Association of Securities Dealers Automated Quotations implies). Level II gives you access to the entire quote board—*all* bids and offers—not just the "Level I" *best* bid and offer. That gives a detailed picture of the entire marketplace—the number of dealers and size at each price level—allowing a better feel and more ability to predict which way things are going. If there are a lot of bids close to the inside but few offers, the price is strong and likely to go up.

Level II is a great tool for "close in" active trading and a must for a true day trader. But it is expensive, often driving the monthly cost or commission hurdle to an equivalent of $50 a month or more. They are a big revenue producer for your broker and for NASDAQ itself. Further, Level II is highly dynamic and requires a lot of attention to follow—not good for someone with other things to do. Still, it gives much greater insight into the current and future behavior of certain stocks, and is a strong nice-to-have at least for the more "active" active investor. Further, it is good for all active investors to understand it—even if they don't use it—in order to have an idea of what goes on behind the scenes. Note that there is no practical quivalent as yet for NYSE or other "listed" stocks.

Charting

Good charting packages have become pretty much a standard offering among online brokers; the service offered by Yahoo!Finance is also very good for the price (free!). Charts provide that picture "worth a thousand words"—or, in this case, data points. They give a pictorial view of the collective behavior defining the price performance and trading pattern of an investment. They also allow quick comparison between stocks, stocks and sectors, and stocks and the market. The more advanced charting packages, which are available through most of the converged trading platforms, aid with technical analysis. They offer basic and some fancy technical tools such as moving averages, Bollinger bands, and "MACD" indicators (more on those in Chapter 11). More advanced packages offer streaming charts, updating the chart automatically as things change. This nice-to-have feature is more power than most active investors need, but a basic charting package with moving averages and other indicators is important.

Fast Execution and Direct Access

For making trades, what once took the filling out of forms, vacuum tubes, and telephone calls can now be done electronically and almost instantaneously. Brokerage services, most of which trade electronically through intermediaries, offer "5-second guarantees" and some go as low as one second for order execution. Some day trading strategies require this kind of execution, where traders make money off of very small price fluctuations or even the spread between bid and offer prices. For the typical active investor, the difference between a one-second and a ten-second execution is not that important; if an investment is a good idea, it is bound to be such ten seconds later! Direct access goes even a step further, where investors are allowed to post their own trades directly into the marketplace with no intermediaries, and to trade with specific market makers. Most active investors do not need direct access and should not place too much weight on execution times. That said, if an investor has bad experiences with slow executions or badly missing price points, a change might be in order.

Low Commissions

Obviously it depends on how active you are, but low commissions are a near-must. The effort to squeeze a little extra return out of your investments should not be compromised by high commissions, and investment decisions should be free of concern about high commissions. The cost of $29.95 for a stock trade—the standard offered by many major players—is the maximum that should be paid. Further, commissions on option trading should be reasonable—$5 or $10 plus $1 per contract is typical. Some brokers offer low commissions on stocks but make it up with high option trading commissions.

Telephone Trading

The ability to trade by telephone through "Telebroker" (Schwab) or a similar service is a must. Active investors are on the go and doing other things, and they must be able to get quotes or trade while in the car, on a commuter train, etc. Commissions should be the same or similar to Internet-based trades—if they aren't, watch out. Some level of telephone support should be available, and full 24/7 coverage is better. There are times (though usually rarely) when the active investor needs help, from account issues to specific questions about certain securities to backup trade capability in an emergency—such as when traveling overseas. Better services offer special sets of agents to help these more sophisticated investors.

Margin and Margin Services

Whether to use margin—to borrow money—to invest is a matter of personal taste and risk preference. The use of margin is generally not necessary to achieve active investing objectives, but having the capability in store to enter a larger short-term position to capture a ripe opportunity does come in handy. The amount an investor can borrow is regulated by the Federal Reserve. Interest rates don't vary a lot between brokers but many have different break points—that is—lower rates for larger amounts.

Option Trading

The use of equity options, mainly to hedge investment positions and generate short-term income, will be discussed in Chapter 14. The trading platform you choose should provide the resources to select and transact option trades. Complete and easily accessed "option chains" (lists of options for a security) and option value modeling through the standard "Black-Scholes" option valuation model are good to have, as are favorable option commission schedules. As a new investor you will need to execute an option agreement. This isn't difficult to do, but it is worth reading the fine print.

A Few Final Words

The active investor has many sources of information at his or her fingertips, from the Internet to print resources. That said, trading platforms can offer still more. At the time of writing, the offerings are fairly standardized—Standard & Poor's Stock Reports, Argus investment reports, and an assortment of analyst reports brought in from elsewhere. It's worth a look, but there isn't much here to differentiate one service from another. Some brokers, like Schwab, offer their own recommendations, although these may be based on other services, like Standard & Poor's. Keep in mind also that there are many, many eyes looking at the same information. Finally, there are also "stock screeners" to help you select stocks on various sets of criteria—some of these are more flexible and work better than others.

As an active investor, you will evolve your own technique, and in that process you will determine the information and execution "windows" that best serve your needs at a preferred cost. From here, we switch gears to examine in detail what you will look at through these windows. Chapter 7 gives a deeper tour through some of the macro factors—the economic cycle and the economic indicators released each month. Chapters 8 and 9 change the perspective to micro, with an explanation of how to use value principles to select businesses and equity investments. Chapters 10 through 12 change the approach from fundamental value to trading and trade timing—how to spot short-term opportunities and capitalize on them. Chapter 13 examines managed investments and fund investing, including Exchange Traded Funds and customized portfolios. Chapter 14 examines attractive specialized investments, including equity and index options and commodities. Finally, Chapter 15 shows how to blend it all together into your own personal active investing style.

Chapter 7

Economic Indicators and the Business Cycle

Once you learn to think like an active investor, and know which investing "windows" to use, the next logical step is to identify what to *watch* through those windows. Every investor will establish his/her own repertoire of "macro" factors influencing the economy and the markets as a whole, and a set of "micro" factors influencing the fortunes of their individual businesses, and thus individual stocks. This chapter opens with the important economic and business activity factors that every active investor should track, and finishes by examining the business cycle and its influence on your investments.

Economic Indicators

Government agencies and private institutions track literally hundreds of pieces of economic data to monitor the pulse of business and the U.S. and world economy. From these tiny bits of data comes a variety of economic and business indicators, typically released monthly, that depict where the economy is and where it is going. (In fact, it's the *change* in the figures that's most important to investors.) As an active investor you should track and be familiar with twenty-five key "numbers" released in each month's economic calendar. While there are many ways to group these numbers, for this book they are grouped as follows:

- *Pure economic indicators* track the level of activity and health of the economy as a whole, including such figures as unemployment and gross domestic product. The three types of measures that follow are all subsets or components of these broader economic indicators.
- *Business activity measures* monitor the level of wholesale or retail private business activity, overall or in specific business sectors.
- *Construction measures* monitor housing and general construction figures.
- *Inflation measures* track prices and productivity at a wholesale and consumer level.

While these measures do not provide great amount of detail at this level, they do provide a well-rounded view of the overall economy and business performance.

Pure Economic Indicators

Pure economic indicators track performance of the economy as a whole. Most of these reports are compiled by the U.S. Department of Commerce, the Federal Reserve, or the Department of Labor. Employment reports, in particular, carry a lot of weight for investors. Why? Because not only do they reflect current economic health, but they are also leading indicators of prosperity (if healthy) or inflation (if employment is *too* strong).

Consumer Confidence

A nonprofit organization known as the Conference Board does a monthly survey of 5,000 households to measure consumer confidence. The resulting index, released the last Tuesday of each month, compiles their feelings about their current situation and their appraisal of the future. Major shifts in the index can foretell future business activity. The similar University of Michigan Consumer Sentiment Index is released twice a month as a preliminary and final reading for the month. Both measures are considered reasonably accurate and important by the investing community.

Consumer Credit

Compiled by the Federal Reserve, Consumer Credit—a slight misnomer—actually measures the amount of consumer *debt*, dividing it into auto, revolving (credit card), and "other." Consumer Credit can be a leading indicator of future consumer spending; if it is high and growing rapidly, it may signal a cooling off in consumer spending. But the tie between debt levels and consumer spending patterns has proven weak, and many market watchers—and the market in general—seem to ignore this report. In addition, the report is released relatively late in the reporting cycle at the fifth day of the month for two months prior.

Employment

The all-important employment report garners headlines in most media outlets. Compiled by the Bureau of Labor Statistics of the Department of Labor and released the first Friday of each month for the month prior, the report is actually compiled from a survey of 60,000 households and 375,000 businesses. The household survey establishes the well-known unemployment rate, while the business survey produces nonfarm payrolls, the average workweek, average hourly earnings, and other figures. Payrolls are further broken down into sectors, including manufacturing, construction, government, and services. These figures are considered strong indicators of the health of those sectors and their future growth prospects, as they show the collective decisions made by managers in these sectors toward hiring, and more generally, where we are in the business cycle. Declines in manufacturing employment figures made headlines during the past few years, both for their take on economic health and their reflection of the more political issue of outsourcing.

Gross Domestic Product (GDP)

Gross Domestic Product, the total value of all goods and services produced in the economy, is the broadest current measure of economic activity. Data is compiled for each calendar quarter by the U.S. Department of Commerce and released the third or fourth week of the month following that quarter. Revisions follow in subsequent months. GDP is broken down into consumption, investment, net exports, government purchases, and inventories, with consumption being the largest component (about two-thirds). A closer look at inventories and net exports tells whether GDP really reflects economic growth or simply a change in inventories or net exports. While GDP indications are moderately important, it is mainly a lagging indicator and active investors should look more closely at smaller units of business activity for signs of where the puck is going.

Initial Claims

Compiled by the Department of Labor, Initial Claims tracks the number of new unemployment benefits claims, thus giving a short-term signal of future economic direction. These numbers are released weekly and are highly volatile; active investors should look for large and sustained moves, usually 30,000 to

50,000 in either direction, as a meaningful underlying trend. Initial claims can produce short-term market swings, but the more complete employment reports usually determine long-term market direction.

International Trade

Trade balance figures are released by the Department of Commerce, usually during the third week of the month for two months prior. They show how well the U.S. economy is faring competitively on the world stage. Exports, reported as a component of the balance, are an important signal of growth in the U.S. economy and of the effects of the current value of the dollar. If exports are declining, it suggests a further fall in the dollar, brought on by market forces or by Fed action—sometimes a decrease in interest rates. If imports are increasing, that may signal an imminent increase in interest rates to cool demand. Rising import numbers also reflect poorly on the competitiveness of American goods and services, which is not good news for industries that must compete on the world stage, such as autos or capital equipment. These reports can have a strong short-term negative effect on the market if their results are unfavorable.

Leading Indicators

More of a news item than a true market mover, the Leading Indicators index is a composite of other figures already released, including employment, construction, and stock price data. It is released by the Conference Board, usually in the first week of the month for two months prior. There is usually no additional specific meaning of this figure for the active investor, but it does act as a summary read for the current business climate.

Personal Income and Consumption

Released by the Department of Commerce, Personal Income measures individual income from all sources including employment, rental income, government transfer payments, and investment income. PI is a good indicator of future demand, and since wages and salaries make up most of it, it is closely tied to employment. Declining PI usually signals a recession, particularly if coincident with weakness in business activity. Personal Consumption Expenditures, or PCE, measures expenditures in three categories: durables, nondurables, and services. Market watchers look at retail sales figures, which come out sooner, so PCE is not a strong market mover, yet it still bears watching for the active investor.

Business Activity Measures

Business activity measures "drill down" into specific components of the economy to assess actual and expected business activity. Such business activity reflects sales to consumers and to other businesses, as well as the buildup or drawdown of inventory.

Auto and Truck Sales

Released by the Department of Commerce, this monthly report measures sales of domestic vehicles, usually heavily tied to interest rates and consumer confidence. The importance of this report as an economic determinant has declined in recent years as the influence of auto manufacturing on the whole economy has waned (mostly due to the growth of the service-based as opposed to the goods-based economy). However, active investors who are investing in the auto industry, as well as other durable goods industries, should still take note of the report.

Business Inventories

Changes in business inventories are important for the active investor. Building inventory can be a good thing if coming off a low, for it is a sign of stronger economic activity and investment. But if inventories grow above normal levels, that can be a sign of declining demand and poor business performance in months ahead. Thus, it isn't just the change, but rather the starting point *and* the change that are important. The Department of Commerce, through its Census Bureau, reports Business Inventories by the fifteenth of each month for two months prior. This is a bit late, but other reports on manufacturing and wholesale inventories usually hit the market first. The BI report does provide useful new data on retail inventories.

Durable Goods

Reported by the Census Bureau of the Department of Commerce, Durable Goods measures the dollar volume of orders, shipments, and unfilled orders (backlog) of durable goods. Durable goods are defined as goods with an intended lifespan of at least three years—cars, appliances, machinery, etc. Orders are a leading indicator, and can be broken down into industries. The number can be distorted by large defense and aircraft orders, but these can be separated out. Orders for capital goods—goods used in business—are another important indicator not only of short-term business activity but also of how businesses look at their future prospects. If you are investing in businesses producing durable goods or capital equipment used by other businesses, then you want to watch this report.

Factory Orders

Also released by the Census Bureau, Factory Orders covers Durable Goods plus orders for nondurable goods—consumer household products, food, and others. It's a more complete view of the economy, but perhaps a less pure indicator of where things are going than the more sensitive Durable Goods report. The Factory Orders report also includes a factory inventory figure, usually the first inventory figure released each month. FO is released the first business day with data from two months prior; it is not especially important in and of itself, but it is used with other reports as part of the economic picture.

National Association of Purchasing Managers (NAPM) Survey

The National Association of Purchasing Managers, a nonprofit industry trade association, releases results of a survey on the first business day of each month taken during the prior month. The survey captures the purchasing plans of a large number of purchasing managers nationwide in an assortment of industries and covers a number of topics: new orders, production, employment plans, inventories, delivery times, prices, and import/export activity. It is a good ground-level read of near-term business activity, and, most importantly for the active investor, it is one of the "freshest" pieces of data (since most government business activity data lags by at least a month) and is easy to read. A figure above 50 percent implies expansion in the coming month, while a number below 50 percent implies contraction. Active investors—particularly those in the manufacturing sector—should watch this report.

Regional Manufacturing Surveys

There is an assortment of surveys done in different parts of the country by other purchasing management organizations and by some of the regional Federal Reserve banks. The Philadelphia Federal Reserve survey comes out first, usually during the third week of the month being reported. The Chicago Purchasing Managers

Index—PMI—is released the last business day of each month and is one of the most widely followed indices of manufacturing activity, coming from this manufacturing-intensive town. Others arrive at various times of the month, but usually follow the more widely used NAPM survey. Like the NAPM survey, the Chicago PMI is presented in the easy-to-read above-below 50 percent format.

Retail Sales

Released by the Census Bureau (Department of Commerce), Retail Sales is taken as a strong indicator of economic health. It reflects consumer behavior and confidence but also the strength of upcoming inventory replenishment which is particularly relevant to the active investor who is investing in retail businesses. As retail sales also reflects auto sales and general price increases, discerning watchers will want to filter out these effects to identify underlying trends. The report comes out relatively early, usually the thirteenth of the month for the month prior.

Construction Measures

Bridging the gap between pure economic and business activity indicators is a set of reports that measure construction and real estate activity. Construction activity *reflects* business and consumer confidence, interest rates, and *predicts* employment and future business activity. Increases in construction also greatly influence sectors such as mortgage lending, building materials, and home improvement. However, keep in mind that the economic influence of construction and furnishing of homes and business establishments spreads widely into other goods and services—such as appliances, furniture, tools, construction equipment, and such. Active investors should watch closely for signs of strength, and particularly of *change* in construction activity.

Construction Spending

Released by the Census Bureau on the first business day of each month for two months prior, Construction Spending shows new residential, nonresidential and public construction. The figures are volatile so individual numbers don't have much impact, but visible trends over three months or more can be important, particularly if you invest in industries closely tied to construction.

Existing Home Sales

Each month the National Association of Realtors releases this report that reflects housing demand, which is itself largely a response to current interest rate policy. This report also shows median home prices by region and home inventories. Home purchases reflect consumer optimism, and the economic impact of home price appreciation is subject to some debate. Many investors look at home price appreciation as a negative for the stock market because (1) money is being taken out of stocks to buy the homes, and (2) it shows a public preference as to where people would like to invest their money. However, reviving home sales after a period of weakness can signal emergence from a recession. Declining home sales can be either a reflection of higher interest rates or sagging consumer incomes and confidence—or both. The report is released around the twenty-fifth of each month for the month prior.

New Home Sales

While existing home sales is released by the National Association of Realtors, New Home Sales is released by the Census Bureau. In terms of measuring consumer confidence and the effect of interest rates, the "read" of this number is much the same as for existing home sales. However, since new homes require more labor and building material, the downstream effects of strong new home sales are worth watching for the active investor. New Home Sales are released the last business day of the month for the month prior. Housing Starts and Building Permits figures, also from the Census Bureau, are leading indicators of New Home Sales and are released earlier usually at the middle of the month. Ordinarily these signals aren't too strong for investors, but for those actively investing in related industries or watching interest rates closely, monitoring these figures is a smart strategy.

Inflation Measures

Few economic phenomena affect the investment world—and are watched with more interest—than inflation. Inflation is the depreciation of currency—money—vis-à-vis the goods and services that it buys. Most economists and investors agree that a *modest* and *consistent* amount of inflation is a good thing—usually in a 2 to 3 percent annual range. While the idea of deflation—falling prices—sounds like a good thing, it actually leads to a dreaded vicious cycle. People delay purchasing decisions expecting lower prices, which in turn leads to lower demand—and more falling prices. Thus, the Federal Reserve—the chief inflation "watchdog"—will go to great lengths to avoid deflation.

Strong inflation is also bad as erodes the value of fixed investments—bonds—since they will be paid back with cheaper dollars later. It also can lead an upward spiral: People expecting higher prices in the future will buy now, causing more dollars to chase the same amount of goods and services, and bringing on still more inflation. There are two types of inflation, and investors should look for signs of both:

Demand-pull inflation occurs when the strength of demand, brought by low interest rates, high income and employment, strong export demand, or any combination of other similar factors causes more dollars to chase the same amount of supply. Shortages crop up, and sellers of goods and services take advantage of the seller's market to raise prices. Demand-pull inflation can be good in the short run for some businesses, as it allows them to raise prices. Eventually, the Federal Reserve will step in to dampen demand-pull inflation by raising interest rates, as it did in the 1999–2000 period. Demand-pull inflation is relatively easy to interpret and control.

Cost-push inflation occurs when shortages of key economic inputs like energy or other natural resources appear, and the resulting price increases in those inputs cause a downstream chain reaction in the economy. The chain reaction is stronger in some parts of the economy than others. The oil price shocks of the 1970s are the best example, and in 2004 the U.S. economy entered another period of raw material price increases. Since the Fed has no control over specific economic inputs (other than the supply of money itself), cost-push inflation is relatively difficult to control, as many who remember the late 1970s may recall. Raising interest rates to control cost-push inflation only leads to "stagflation," a particularly challenging environment of price increases among a climate of economic decline.

Given how sensitive the market is to the effects of inflation, active investors should watch the indicators in the following four sections:

Consumer Price Index (CPI)

Released mid-month by the Bureau of Labor Statistics, the well-known CPI measures the price level of a fixed basket of consumer goods and services. CPI is widely used as the strongest overall indicator of inflation in the economy. However, the active investor should keep in mind that there are some flaws in the report; for example, it does not include many big-ticket items, including technology products, and the figures are often reported with and without food and energy components, which may dramatically understate true consumer inflation impact and "experience." The CPI without the more volatile food and energy components is known as the "core rate" of inflation. Monthly changes in CPI and the annual inflation rate implied by the monthly CPI change should be watched closely. Not only are actual changes in inflation patterns important, but public and government *perception* of those changes can also be critical for the future direction of interest rates and spending patterns.

Producer Price Index (PPI)

Released slightly before CPI each month, also by the Bureau of Labor Statistics, the PPI measures prices at the wholesale level, and is looked at as a leading indicator of consumer (CPI) inflation.

Employment Cost Index

Particularly in a demand-pull inflationary environment, active investors must watch the employment cost index and its components. An overheated economy will show itself in the number of hours of overtime worked, average hourly labor costs, and overall wage rates. The ECI can signal emergence from a recession, as length of workweek and overtime tells of greater output before firms decide to actually hire more employees. ECI is released by the Bureau of Labor Statistics quarterly, usually at the end of the first month after the end of the quarter.

Specific Commodity Prices

Active investors should track prices of at least a few key commodities—for example, the price of ubiquitous economic inputs such as oil and other forms of energy, and the prices of other commodities related to their interests. The price of electricity, basic foodstuffs, lumber, and other commodities can affect the performance of specific businesses drawing heavily on those inputs. Own Starbucks? Might be a good idea to watch the price of coffee. Airlines are particularly sensitive to oil prices, and homebuilders use a lot of lumber—you get the idea. "Spot" (current) and futures prices for individual commodities appear in financial newspapers and the Commodity Research Bureau calculates an index of commodity prices published in most financial newspapers and on the PBS Nightly Business Report.

The Economic, Business, and Market Cycle

The economic cycle, while not a perfect market forecaster, foretells the short-term performance of most stocks as a whole. Closer study reveals that many industries and sectors behave differently depending on the point on the business cycle. Since most players are trying to predict the future, the market tends to anticipate economic cycles, and individual sectors will tend to beat or lag the market.

The figure on the next page depicts the simultaneous behavior of the economy, interest rates, the stock market, and individual market sectors. By necessity it is somewhat oversimplified, and while these behaviors are fairly predictable, their timing may not be. Recessions, recoveries, and transitions can vary in length, and interest rate changes and the market "forecast" may not always occur as predicted or when predicted.

A picture is worth a thousand words:

Economic and Market Cycles

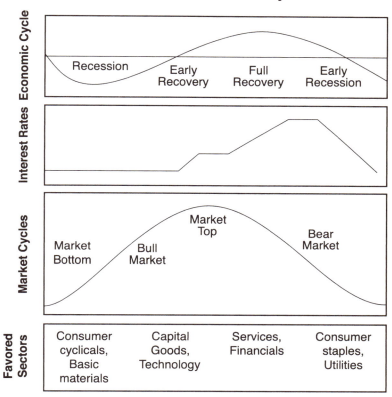

Recession and Early Recession

Recession is usually defined by economists as two or more successive quarters of negative growth as defined by Gross Domestic Product, or GDP. Markets anticipate recession through declining business activity, high inventories resulting from low demand, weakening personal income, rising unemployment, and a host of other factors. They then begin to sell investments, creating a bear market before the recession actually shows up in the numbers. The period from late 2000 to mid-2001 is an example. The Federal

Reserve sees the same indicators that the markets do but may wait for more or stronger signals before reducing interest rates to jumpstart the economy.

During early bear markets, so-called "recession-proof" or defensive stocks get favor. Consumer staples such as food and low-priced consumables like clothing and books are among the last thing to be cut from budgets, so food stocks like J.M. Smucker and Hershey tend to fare well during this period, while makers of "big ticket" items like autos or travel services suffer. Defense contractors and other government suppliers tend to do well. Demand for utility services remains strong, while declining interest rates usually favor these capital-intensive businesses. As the recession hits bottom, investors see some light for conventional cyclical and basic materials industries, like chemicals, forest products, glass, and mining.

Early and Full Recovery

Active investors should keep in mind that recessions are usually short-lived unless major political or economic events—like 9/11 or the Watergate scandal—reduce consumer or business confidence for longer periods. Reduced interest rates stimulate demand, as the cost of money (cost of capital, for businesses) is cheaper and it makes more economic sense to make more purchases sooner. The recession and its period of declining or uncertain income causes pent-up demand—that is, demand for goods and services delayed through the recessionary period. Consumers regain confidence and start buying, which in turn becomes business demand. Businesses respond to this demand by increasing inventories and buying capital equipment to increase capacity or make existing capacity more productive. As signs of recovery start to build, demand for business capital goods grows, and business and more economically liberated consumers begin to demand technology products. Demand for these products and general inventory buildup create strength in other sectors of the economy. Once in full recovery, indicators like GDP growth, employment, business output, commodity and labor prices, and a host of other indicators are usually topping out. Moreover, it becomes obvious on the street, with such signs as more commuter traffic, hotel room shortages, and long lines at nearby restaurants. But savvy investors, looking for what's ahead, see a scenario of contracting manufacturing demand (remember the "dreaded diamond effect" from Chapter 1?) and, once the economy "breaks" and heads lower, a cycle of declining interest rates. Declining interest rates help financial institutions, for they tend to borrow short term at low rates and lend for longer terms for higher rates. Beware that a *sharp* decline like that seen in 2000–01 can raise credit risk (bankruptcies, late payments, etc.), making financial stocks a riskier play.

The natural economic cycle is fairly predictable, and clearly the more predictable it is the better. The gentle cycles of the 1950s, 1960s, and early 1990s were relatively easy to follow. More recently cycles have become more extreme, driven by world events, access to real-time information, and, just perhaps, by the fact that everyone is now watching. It is never good to invest without thinking, so attention to economic cycles serves to enhance the active investor's thought process—not to replace it.

Part III:

The Quest for Value

Chapter 8

Value Investing for Today's Investor

Value investing? The last you heard, this was the buy-it-and-hold-it-forever approach made popular by Warren Buffett and his disciples. Choose a few mundane companies like carpet and paint manufacturers, plunk down a few thousand bucks, and wait. And wait and wait. What does that have to do with active investing, you might ask? Quite simply, any investor choosing to commit capital to a company (or any other investment, for that matter) should understand the fundamentals of that business, and to invest at a favorable price. The value approach produces the best long- and short-term opportunities and minimizes risk for the time-constrained active investor. While the traditional long-term value investing approach works as-is for foundation investments, this chapter goes beyond to teach you how to think like a value investor across your entire portfolio, short-term investments and trades included.

Value—The Long and Short of It

Traditional value investors focus on the long term. They seek fundamentally good, sound businesses judged on past performance and future prospects. Fundamentalists consider financial, marketplace, and management factors and how those factors are deployed to achieve shareowner value. Value investors like solid financials and steady income and growth prospects, all wrapped in a package with strong marketplace position and a trustworthy management team. They seek businesses they can understand and businesses that don't change much or that have control over changes impacting them. They seek uniquely unassailable market positions—that is, companies with figurative "moats" around their core business, competitive barriers making it difficult for other companies to steal their turf. Finally, they seek to buy into those businesses at a reasonable long-term price, though they may pay a seemingly high price in the short term. Traditional value investors favor companies like Coca-Cola, which sells a high-margin product to an eternally captive group of customers, and has a brand name and reputation that no amount of invested capital could replace.

Traditional value investors are patient. They focus on potential long-term return of the business and aren't much concerned with next quarter's earnings or even the ebb and flow of the economy. And they certainly aren't concerned with short-term stock price fluctuations. This isn't to say that they launch a "buy" order and simply walk away—these investors constantly watch for fundamental business changes in their companies. When industry fundamentals change or if they lose trust in management, they quickly move on.

It's About Investing in a Business

The value investor's underlying premise: They are investing in a business. They treat the investment process as though they were buying the business itself—the *whole* business. Value investors view any investment as a commitment of capital to an enterprise in exchange for an eventual healthy return on that investment—and a return worth the risk. Return-on-investment, growth-at-a-reasonable-price, and buy and hold (but not blind trust) are value-investing mantras. Value investors fully *appraise* any business they invest in.

There has been plenty written on the cunning style and approach of the mid-twentieth century genius Benjamin Graham (*The Intelligent Investor* is his classic book) and his student, Warren Buffett. Both men practice much the same thing, except that Graham was more interested in underpriced assets—where the value of a company's stock underestimated their true value. Buffett, on the other hand, recognized that determining true asset value is too difficult (and hasn't *that* become more true in recent years?). Instead, future profit-growth prospects, driven by sustainable competitive advantage and business growth, are most important. Both men are essentially drinking from the same glass; asset value and profit-producing potential should be, at day's end, much the same thing.

Darn, That's Cheap

That the value investing approach has merit for more active parts of portfolio is a key active investing premise. Opportunism is important, and the prudent active investor keeps tabs on a list of companies with good fundamentals—financials, marketplace fundamentals, and management teams—that they would like to own eventually. Active investors are bargain hunters, and when something appears cheap in the marketplace, they consider action.

Sometimes the market gets so caught up in short-term emotion that it distorts or misjudges the value of individual companies within. The active investor is ready to pounce sometimes for the short term, sometimes for a lot longer. Is this investing? You bet it is. In clear contrast to speculation, the active investor employs business rationale, takes time to evaluate the fundamentals, and decides the opportunity is worth the risk for the capital invested—whether for five minutes or five years.

That Which Creates Value

Business value can be most simply defined as a return on an investment. "Return" can be further qualified by amount, timing, and probability—that is, how much, how soon, and how likely is the return? A high probability of a large cash return in a short period of time is obviously worth more than a modest probability of a small return that won't be collected for years. Rational investors in any business—whether a *Fortune* 500 company or a nearby espresso stand—examine the fundamental capability of a business to produce large cash returns soon and with as little risk as possible.

Here's where it gets tricky. How do you know for sure that a business will produce these returns, large, steady, and soon? The answer is: You can't. But just as you would find when evaluating a car, a school, or a vacation destination, there are certain hard facts to consider about a business—as well as subjective or nonquantifiable factors that can be applied in addition to the cold, hard facts. With a business, hard facts are represented by financial statements. Financial statements are a report card of the actual past performance of a business. Thus, future financial performance can be projected or estimated by drawing upon past data, but like driving a car by looking at the rear view mirror, the past doesn't always predict the future. So one must look at factors that foretell financial performance and add them to the business appraisal. What factors should be looked at? The less tangible factors of marketplace performance, operational strategy, and—last but not least—management effectiveness all drive future financials, and thus all are part of the value equation. Only by assessing all of these factors can we get a true handle on the future prospects of the business.

Financials

For our purposes in this book (and your purposes as an active investor), it's impossible to do a thorough treatment of financial analysis. However, this book does offer some theoretical and practical highlights to enable you to see certain financial things more clearly. As an active investor, you don't want (nor do you have the time) to become a full-time financial analyst, so this guide will stick to the basics, enabling you to make your appraisal effective for the time spent. The first topic is a more theoretical construct of financial value known as *intrinsic value,* the second is a more practical explanation of the use of financial statements to assess financial value.

Intrinsic Value

Intrinsic value is a scary-sounding term representing a fundamental fact of business and investing: the "real" worth of any investment is the "present value" of all future returns—nothing more and nothing less. It makes sense when you think about it—the only real value of an investment is *what you'll get out of it*—the *return*—now or someday. It doesn't matter what form it takes—whether it comes as steady payout of income as dividends, or much later as a refund of your capital with an added return. What *does* matter is *how much* return and *when*.

You are probably familiar with the *time value of money* concept; in other words, a dollar today is worth more than a dollar received a year, five years, or twenty years from now. *How much* more is a function of how much that dollar could earn doing something else, a concept known as *opportunity cost*. If the alternate opportunity is a risk-free return from a U.S. Treasury bond paying 5 percent per year, then a dollar received next year could be considered to be worth 5 percent less, or 95 cents, and for each year after that, it is worth sequentially 5 percent less. That 5 percent is known as the *discount rate*. Five percent taken off sequentially for five years, or (.95 * .95 * .95 * .95 * .95) brings that dollar down to 77 cents. That same dollar, brought back as return twenty years from now, is worth ($1 * [.95^{20}]$), or 36 cents—an almost two-thirds decline in its value. Note the obvious: The further out you go, or the higher the alternative return—the less that future dollar is worth.

Intrinsic value "science" requires projecting future returns and the timing of those returns, and then applying an appropriate discount rate. The total return is represented by a set of yearly cash flows followed by a final, or "terminal," cash flow when the investment is sold some years later. The "art" is in projecting the size and timing of these flows and deciding the appropriate discount rate.

Sophisticated financiers do this kind of projection all the time, but, in practice, it beyond most time-constrained investors. It is simply too hard to project these returns with any degree of accuracy. However the concept of intrinsic value has merit for active investors. Active investors are well served to think of investments in terms of future cash flow, whether the future is long or short term. A business that can't generate predictable future cash flow, or that only promises to do so some years into the future, is a less attractive investment. One that produces more cash sooner and more dependably is worth more.

Growth

Growth is a key intrinsic value driver. A steady return of a dollar each year means less and less as time goes on—but what if that return grows every year? What if the growth exceeds the discount rate depreciation? In that scenario, the intrinsic value—and thus the investment value—is much higher. Essentially, the company is doing more with your capital than you can yourself by buying Treasury bonds, and that's good.

But What About Risk?

Is an investment in a high-flying technology start-up treated the same as an investment in a steady supplier of corn syrup? Does the intrinsic value look the same? Not even close. The risk of loss, and the variability and timing of returns, is much less predictable with the technology start-up. Thus, to justify an investment, you would want a larger return. Stated differently, the return required to get you to part with capital would be higher than what is reflected in the discount rate. The theoretical discount rate applied to calculate intrinsic value would be higher, driving down the value of future returns. They are less predictable, and so worth less when looking through today's spyglass into the future. Thus, the price you'd be willing to pay for the stock is lower. Only if the technology company's growth rate far outstrips the necessarily higher discount rate does the high flyer get consideration.

Armed with the conceptual framework of intrinsic value, the active investor can make a first judgment of a company's prospects. A company with strong cash flow and strong growth proven in the short term, and having few long-term uncertainties, is preferred over one with an unproven business model and only a hope of achieving growth. The intrinsic value concept applies not only to businesses but also to investments. The intrinsic value of an investment to you, the investor—whether an individual stock, a fund, or a piece of antique furniture—is equivalent to a time-discounted picture of future cash flows paid during ownership and finalized at disposal. Do active investors sit with calculators estimating the intrinsic value of Starbucks while sipping their lattes? Probably not, but it's the concept that counts. More returns, made sooner and with more predictability, mean the business has greater value, and thus is a greater value for the investment.

The intrinsic value concept applies to the business as a whole, for as an owner, you will reap the returns from the whole business. But the savvy active investor also looks at the intrinsic value of key parts of the business. For a company like Hewlett-Packard, the printing component of the business, with its steady and cumulatively growing cash flow from its high-margin ink business, has high intrinsic value. The PC portion of the business, however, has weak and unpredictable cash flows and very low cash flows for the amount of capital invested. The server portion is somewhere in between but closer to the PC business. Does the company as a whole have a high intrinsic value? It's a tossup. Similarly, FedEx (Federal Express) has the familiar high-margin, hard-to-duplicate small package express business returning decent cash flow when fuel prices are moderate. But they are expanding into the lower-margin trucking business—what does this do to total intrinsic value? It is almost predictable as Newton's Second Law of Thermodynamics that companies strive to achieve growth by expanding into lower-margin businesses. They may increase revenues, but strength and predictability of cash flow returns suffer, thus moderating intrinsic value. Remember, the business whole is the sum of many parts.

Points to Remember

- Think of a stock as a share of a business, and think of buying the stock as buying the business.
- When buying shares, think in terms of intrinsic value. It isn't necessary to run the all the numbers, but think of an investment in terms of its short and long-term returns, and consider whether those returns are worth the current price.

Chapter 9

Appraising a Business: A Value Approach

Reading financial reports is, for most investors, an exercise in mandated patience—a polite way of saying they're dull and boring. Indeed, financial statements are a dry, factual reporting—an accounting—of the dollar results of business activity.

Once relegated to the quiet realm of the few value-oriented investors interested during the go-go years, financial statements have returned to center stage. Why? First, financial statements have been the subject of egregious manipulations designed to hide negative facts and, worse, enrich unscrupulous managers. Secondly, more investors, burned by hype and hope, are bringing fundamentals back into the equation.

The accounting for business activity and the preparation of statements has been largely a science governed by standards set by the Financial Accounting Standards Board (FASB), an association of professional accountants. The key word is "largely." Specific rules govern the valuation and timing of revenue, expenses, assets, and liabilities. But in many cases these rules are not absolute and can be creatively interpreted by accountants and managers to suit a business situation. It's not too hard to value cash assets, securities, buildings, or equipment, but how does one account for the value of a brand? Or an acquired company? If a company sells a product and a three-year service agreement to go with it, when and how is that revenue booked? And what about the research and development expenses (if indeed, that's what they really were)? What about stock options, where companies give away potential equity capital (that could have been sold for a higher price) to employees without booking an expense?

Thus today's investors, and active investors in particular, should look at financial statements with a grain of salt, recognizing that there is some latitude in crafting them. That said, they do provide an essential barometer of business performance, particularly when compared with preceding statements issued by the same firm. Essentially there are three financial statements to pay attention to.

Owned and Owed: The Balance Sheet

The *balance sheet* accounts for a firm's assets (properties it owns), liabilities (amounts it owes others), and capital (the equity, or investment, of its owners). The assets in place are financed by a mix of owner's equity and capital furnished by others (liabilities), thus the basic accounting equation: Assets = Liabilities + Capital. Assets are further broken down into "current" assets, including cash, securities, accounts receivable, and inventories, which flow through the business, and "fixed" assets—property, plant, and equipment—that physically support the business. There is also an "other," or "intangible," category for assets—like acquired business brand value—that can't be precisely valued. Liabilities are broken down into current liabilities, which fund the short-term operations of the business, and long-term liabilities, which usually but don't always fund business infrastructure. The value investor knows that liabilities—debts—are real, because they are contractually owed to someone else. Assets, on the other hand, especially fixed assets and intangibles, are subjectively valued and may or may not be real. Thus, the value of owner's capital may also be partially subjective. The balance sheet is taken as a snapshot in time.

Ins and Outs: The Income Statement

The *income statement* accounts for the revenue (sales) and expenses of the business. The difference between the two—whether positive or negative—is net profit. Important items include cost of goods sold—the direct cost of the product or service sold—and expenses, which are largely the selling, general, and administrative costs of the business. Depreciation is another important part; it is an accounting charge representing the decline in value of assets, for which there is no cash transaction. The quality or accuracy of an income statement can be compromised by timing issues in recognizing revenue and expenses. The practice of depreciating assets, particularly intangible assets—while heavily regulated by FASB and the IRS—remains an area of flexibility in statement generation. Income statements cover a particular reporting period, usually a quarter or a year.

Cold and Hard: The Cash Flow Statement

The *cash flow statement*, as the name implies, tracks the flow of cash in to and out of the business. It accompanies the income statement but only shows the transactions that involve cash. Since cash returns are most coveted by investors, and since cash flow is subject to little accounting interpretation, cash flow statements are increasingly being relied upon by investors to determine the real health of a business. A business that consumes more cash—more capital—than it produces will not survive in the long run. That said, cash flow statements can be muddied by the timing of major purchases. An airline that buys an airplane will incur a huge cash expense when it is bought, while the accounting treatment of the expense on the income statement is appropriately spread over time by depreciation. Likewise, up and down shifts in inventory, accounts receivable, and payables may distort cash flow statements without any direct effect on income statements. Still, tracking the flow of cash into and out of the business, especially over time, is increasingly important.

Financial Statement Examples

Perfect examples of the three financial statements—balance sheet, income statement, and cash flow statement—are elusive, as many are overly complex or burdened with special "one-time" changes. Presented here are the statements of a midsized company engaged in the business of corrective laser ("Lasik") surgery in retail outlets known as "LCA Vision." LCA trades on the NASDAQ National Market under the symbol "LCAV" and is sort of a retail/technology hybrid. The statements are relatively simple, and, largely on the basis of fundamentals, the company's stock price rose from about 4 in April 2003 to a high (perhaps too high) of 30 and change in April 2004. There were plenty of clues for the sharp value investor to pick up. The stock illustrates several value concepts important to the active investor, and also many trading concepts covered in the next chapter, hence its selection as the example. The figures used in these examples are pulled from the "Financials" section on Yahoo!Finance for ticker symbol LCAV.

Value Tests of Sound Performance

In the necessarily short space below are a few important value tests. While not a complete substitute for thorough business and

Figure 9.1: LCA Vision Cash Flow Statement

Annual Data — All numbers in thousands

PERIOD ENDING	31-Dec-03	31-Dec-02	31-Dec-01
Net Income	7,269	(3,826)	(23,375)
Operating Activities, Cash Flows Provided By or Used In			
Depreciation	6,377	5,997	5,625
Adjustments To Net Income	2,510	230	18,748
Changes In Accounts Receivables	(5,656)	21	2,946
Changes In Liabilities	1,940	2,774	(5,966)
Changes In Inventories	-	-	-
Changes In Other Operating Activities	40	497	29
Total Cash Flow From Operating Activities	**12,480**	**5,693**	**(1,993)**
Investing Activities, Cash Flows Provided By or Used In			
Capital Expenditures	(5,231)	(1,789)	(7,061)
Investments	-	(44)	8,151
Other Cashflows from Investing Activities	95	(202)	615
Total Cash Flows From Investing Activities	**(5,136)**	**(2,035)**	**1,705**
Financing Activities, Cash Flows Provided By or Used In			
Dividends Paid	-	-	-
Sale Purchase of Stock	37,945	(2,217)	(2,976)
Net Borrowings	1,321	(20)	(196)
Other Cash Flows from Financing Activities	-	268	377
Total Cash Flows From Financing Activities	39,266	(1,969)	(2,795)
Effect Of Exchange Rate Changes	-	-	-
Change In Cash and Cash Equivalents	**$46,610**	**$1,689**	**($3,083)**

financial analysis, these tests serve as quick-read indicators of sound business and financial performance.

Does the Firm Produce or Consume Capital?

The first check occurs in the cash flow statement. The issue: Does a business throw off more capital, in the form of cash, than it consumes? Does it constantly have to go to the capital markets (i.e., sell bonds or more stock) to finance its growth? Or worse yet, its day-to-day operations? Companies that are self-funded are best in the long term; that is, they are able to grow their business "organically" by reinvesting capital generated by the business instead of finding more on the outside through borrowing or sale of more stock. Even better—especially if the business exhibits healthy growth anyway—is a company that finances that growth internally and has excess generated capital to spare. The financial world calls this excess capital "free cash flow."

So how do you figure out whether a business produces or consumes capital? On the cash flow statement in **Figure 9.1** there are three categories: Operating Activities, Investing Activities, and Financing Activities. Cash Flow from Operating Activities shows the net cash provided by (or used in, in parenthesis) by the normal daily business operations. Cash Flow from Investing Activities represents cash generated by (used for) investing in the business—i.e., for capital equipment related to the business, or for investments in other businesses. The key is to figure out whether cash generated from operating activities consistently exceeds cash used for investment activities and particularly capital equipment. The successful capital generating business always generates more cash than it uses, and you can see that in the case of LCAV, the situation is positive and improving. Why? The company is (1) becoming more profitable, and (2) gradually slowing down its expansion, requiring less capital. A caveat: Watch out for companies with excessively long capital equipment cycles, like airlines, which may show positive flows for a number of years before having to buy more airplanes, although well-managed airlines will spread this out over time.

Following the Bouncing Dollar

Reading operating cash flow statements is an acquired skill. Using the LCAV example, net income of $7.629 (million) is the starting point, but depreciation and amortizations are added back (since they were income statement expenses but not cash expenses). Changes in the "working capital" items—Accounts Receivable, Accounts Payable, and Inventory—are tricky to follow, but try this: Any number that is positive means there is more cash; any number that is negative means less cash came into the business.

For example, the ($5.656) million Changes In Accounts Receivable means that the company booked that amount in sales, but didn't collect the cash—instead, they financed it for the customer through accounts receivable. Cash didn't decrease, but was effectively used to accomplish this financing. Similarly, the $1.940M added to Accounts Payable reflects expense on the income statement, but LCAV effectively borrowed that from their suppliers through increasing Accounts Payable, which would have meant a cash outflow if paid directly. Most companies have similar transactions for increases and decreases in inventory, but LCAV, a provider of vision care services, effectively has no inventory. The key is to keep track of what is and isn't producing cash. Sustained negatives in Accounts Receivable figures may reveal trouble in terms of having to finance more and more sales. This also shows up as year-over-year Receivables growth on the Balance Sheet.

The immediate lesson, again: LCAV is generating capital and generating it at an increasing rate.

The Financing Category

Finally, on the LCAV cash flow statement, you can see Cash Flow from Financing Activities, which indicates whether or not the business took in more capital from the outside. In 2003, the company sold a number of shares of stock to finance some expansion and for "general corporate purposes." This is not really that important, particularly since it is a one-time event. Companies going to the capital markets again and again are another matter. They are acquiring capital not otherwise generated by the business. Good to see on the LCAV statement is negative flows, or outflows, in the Financing categories in previous years—the company was using capital to buy back shares, effectively enriching existing shareholders. A savvy active investor reviewing this statement would applaud the surplus capital but put a little marker flag next to the Accounts Receivable change and the Sale of Stock to see what followed in the next few statements.

Is the Business Profitable?

Profit is the bottom line for any investment. Without profits there is no return on capital invested, and the theoretical value of the business is zero, notwithstanding future prospects and saleable assets owned. Bottom-line profits can be hard to understand (are they real and sustainable, or one-time successes, or based on accounting tricks?) and even harder to predict.

Gross Margin

So what is an active investor to do? The rational investor trains his/her eye to look at profit margins and the *change* in profit margins. In particular they look at *gross* profit margins, for they represent the clearest picture of core business results. What does the company make, what can they charge, and what does it cost to make? The combined answer to these questions lies in gross

Appraising a Business: A Value Approach

Figure 9.2: LCA Vision Income Statement

Annual Data — All numbers in thousands

PERIOD ENDING	31-Dec-03	31-Dec-02	31-Dec-01
Total Revenue	81,423	61,838	68,096
Cost of Revenue	47,286	41,066	47,242
Gross Profit	34,137	20,772	20,854
Operating Expenses			
Research Development	-	-	-
Selling General and Administrative	20,609	21,150	21,459
Non Recurring	-	(174)	1,774
Others	6,377	5,997	5,625
Total Operating Expenses	-	-	-
Operating Income or Loss	7,151	(6,201)	(8,004)
Income from Continuing Operations			
Total Other Income/Expenses Net	782	2,501	873
Earnings Before Interest And Taxes	7,878	(3,648)	(6,769)
Interest Expense	18	4	17
Income Before Tax	7,860	(3,652)	(6,786)
Income Tax Expense	591	174	16,589
Minority Interest	(372)	(189)	(10)
Net Income From Continuing Ops	7,269	(3,826)	(23,375)
Non-recurring Events			
Discontinued Operations	-	-	-
Extraordinary Items	-	-	-
Effect Of Accounting Changes	-	-	-
Other Items	-	-	-
Net Income	7,269	(3,826)	(23,375)
Preferred Stock And Other Adjustments	-	-	-
Net Income Applicable To Common Shares	$7,269	($3,826)	($23,375)

margin. A growing gross margin is a good sign of a favorable market position—stronger market share and control over product price—and/or favorable control of direct costs of producing the product. Today's airline business is the poster child for poor gross margin performance. Competitive pressure gives little control over price while expensive fuel and labor inputs give little control over costs.

Referring to the LCA Vision income statement **(Figure 9.2)** you can see growing Gross Margins in action. In 2001, it was 30.6 percent ($20,854M cost of revenue divided by $68,096M in gross revenue); in 2002 it rose to 33.6 percent and again to 41.9 percent in 2003, as prices for corrective laser surgery firmed and costs declined. Investors can get a more "granular," or detailed, look by viewing quarterly, instead of annual, statements on Yahoo!Finance. Value Line gives ten years or more of margin and most other information for the companies it follows.

Expenses, Operating and Net Profit Margin

The income statement continues with operating expenses, operating margin, and net profit margin. Operating expenses, which are indirect expenses not tied directly the production of the product or service, indicate how well the company spends money on things like advertising and general administration. "SG&A" is the popular acronym for "Selling, General and Administrative" expenses, the major expenses item for most businesses. How well does the company control these costs? If they rise, do they rise at a rate less than the rise in revenues, indicating more operational efficiency? Operating expenses reveal management effectiveness, organizational efficiency, and control over the selling process and channels. Research and Development, or "R&D", is another important operating expense, though it is not one found in most service businesses.

You can use the LCA Vision income statement example

Appraising a Business: A Value Approach 123

(Figure 9.2) as a lesson on expenses and expense control. In 2001, LCAV booked $21.459M in "Selling, General and Administrative" (SG&A) expenses, or 31.5 percent of total revenue. It actually rose to 34.2 percent in 2002 before declining to 25.3 percent in 2003. Interpretation: (1) for this business, expenses are almost as large as direct costs, which would be expected for a service business (not for a manufacturing business), and (2) these costs are relatively fixed as revenues increase. Indeed, the fact that LCAV did not grow SG&A at all as revenues grew 20 percent is a good sign.

What Is "EBITDA"?

EBITDA—Earnings Before Taxes, Depreciation and Amortization—is a common yardstick of operational performance for investors and company managers alike to assess "controllable" operating results. EBITDA is analogous to operating margin except that it excludes depreciation. As such, EBITDA is also used to approximate cash flow. EBITDA works well as a short-term performance indicator for controllable and changeable business factors. The problem, which is brought on by the exclusion of depreciation, is that it does not account for the cost of capital items—buildings, equipment, etc.—used in the business. An airline relying on EBITDA gets a look at fare sales less fuel and labor costs, but besides routine maintenance the figure in no way accounts for the cost of the airplanes. So EBITDA is better for noncapital intensive businesses like financials, publishing, media, and some retail and service businesses.

Removing operating expenses leaves "operating margin"—a more holistic indicator of business performance, but less of an indicator of market position, pricing power, and the cost of direct inputs into the product. Finally, net profit margin is the true bottom line—after interest expenses, taxes, and so forth. Taxes may be beyond the control of the business, but other items, such as interest costs, are controllable. A company making strides in operating margin but not in net profit may have problems with its capital structure (too much expensive debt) or tax efficiency (which may depend on where it operates). Strides in net margin without corresponding progress in operating margin or expenses may not be sustainable or even real.

Thus, the active investor seeks to understand business profitability and whether it is getting *more* or *less* profitable. This "intrinsic" evaluation is supplemented by peer analysis—how does the company being examined compare to others in that industry?

How "Real" Are the Business Assets?

Internet stocks, Enron, WorldCom, and others have taught investors lessons about many things, including the asset portion of the balance sheet. As stated before, liabilities are always real, while assets may or may not be. Assets can be as real as cash or the critical and desirable business assets necessary to produce and deliver the product. But assets can also include outmoded or unnecessary fixed resources, uncollectible debts, and a variety of accounting assets that may defy reality.

The quality and value of fixed assets on hand also needs to be examined. Investors don't have access to lists of specific assets. But the value of specific-purpose assets, such as railroad tracks, is often less than booked. Meanwhile the value of land is often greater than that booked since it is usually booked at cost instead of market value (all of this makes valuing railroad companies tricky!). Even more importantly, technological progress can render certain assets obsolete or less valuable for the business far faster than depreciation accounts for the decline.

Figure 9.3: LCA Vision Balance Sheet

Annual Data All numbers in thousands

PERIOD ENDING	31-Dec-03	31-Dec-02	31-Dec-01
Assets			
Current Assets			
Cash And Cash Equivalents	64,908	18,298	16,609
Short Term Investments	-	-	-
Net Receivables	4,057	730	751
Inventory	-	-	-
Other Current Assets	1,422	1,462	1,959
Total Current Assets	**70,387**	**20,490**	**19,319**
Long Term Investments	1,134	263	290
Property Plant and Equipment	17,345	18,433	22,658
Goodwill	275	275	275
Intangible Assets	-	-	-
Accumulated Amortization	-	-	-
Other Assets	435	408	646
Deferred Long Term Asset Charges	461	127	-
Total Assets	**90,037**	**39,996**	**43,188**
Liabilities			
Current Liabilities			
Accounts Payable	9,401	7,515	4,915
Short/Current Long Term Debt	-	10	26
Other Current Liabilities	-	-	-
Total Current Liabilities	**9,401**	**7,525**	**4,941**
Long Term Debt	-	-	4
Other Liabilities	963	-	-
Deferred Long Term Liability Charges	457	129	-
Minority Interest	414	230	41
Negative Goodwill	-	-	-
Total Liabilities	**11,235**	**7,884**	**4,986**

Figure 9.3: LCA Vision Balance Sheet (continued)

Annual Data — All numbers in thousands

PERIOD ENDING	31-Dec-03	31-Dec-02	31-Dec-01
Stockholders' Equity			
Misc Stocks Options Warrants	-	-	-
Redeemable Preferred Stock	-	-	-
Preferred Stock	-	-	-
Common Stock	16	13	52
Retained Earnings	(37,069)	(44,338)	(40,512)
Treasury Stock	(15,462)	(15,462)	(13,013)
Capital Surplus	131,203	91,474	91,080
Other Stockholder Equity	114	425	595
Total Stockholder Equity	78,802	32,112	38,202
Net Tangible Assets	$78,527	$31,837	$37,927

Is the Business Becoming More Productive?

Generally a well-managed business (or government or household or any other entity) will learn how to get more output per unit of input invested. Most investors learn how to get more out of a gallon of gas or a gallon of milk in their personal lives; the same should occur in a business, from experience if for no other reason.

Businesses should also capitalize on what economists call "economies of scale." As the size of the business increases, certain inputs or assets can stay relatively the same and still support the business. While LCA Vision may need to open more storefronts to increase its volume of procedures, they shouldn't need much expansion in corporate headquarters. Advertising and other marketing functions become more effective and internal operating improvements can cut the time per procedure and bring more patients through the facility. All of these learning improvements—mixed with technological improvements in equipment and "back-office" processes—should make the business more productive.

Not Always in Clear View

One inherent difficulty with unit productivity figures: there is no SEC or FASB requirement to report them or report them consistently. Companies report them voluntarily, and they may or may not choose to. With some justification, many companies treat these figures as sensitive proprietary information. "Same store sales" has become so much a standard in the retail industry that most companies report it, but many other unit productivity indicators may be hard to find or nonexistent. The more detailed "10-K" annual reports may shed light. Value investors place a high value on "transparency"—that is, the willingness of management teams to share key information with investors—so companies that make their employee and facility counts available score a few points just for having done so.

The enlightened investor looks for productivity clues in two places: in the financials and in "unit productivity" figures. Financial statements can answer questions such as: Does the business bring more revenue per dollar of property, plant, and equipment? Per dollar of current assets? Per dollar of inventory? It's good to examine these figures over time and also comparatively against other companies in similar businesses.

"Unit productivity" measures productivity for nonfinancial business inputs like number of stores, store square footage, or number of employees. "Same store sales" is a favorite for retail—how much business did the firm do per store, particularly for stores open during both periods of comparison? Sales figures by themselves are not as good an indicator, for growth can be achieved simply by opening more stores. Same store sales breaks out the sales per existing store, and it is therefore a better indicator of whether the business is truly selling more stuff to more customers. Similarly, sales per employee indicates whether the business is really doing more with less.

Is the Business Financially Strong?

Thousands of well-paid professionals make such assessments each day. It is hopeless to try to give all the secrets to financial analysis in this treatment, but there are a few quick tests you can use. As you might consider in your own personal finances, does the business live within its means? Is it walking close to the edge? Or moving toward firmer ground? Whether the company is producing or consuming capital, as covered above, is a good place to start, but there is more to consider.

Too Much Debt?

The presence of debt gives a company "financial leverage"; that is, more assets can be owned, bringing proportionately greater returns per dollar of owner's capital. However, this quickly becomes a two-edged sword if the business starts to lose money. Additionally, the firm must pay the interest. So the amount of debt and particularly long-term debt should be considered. How big is the debt compared to total capital? A capital structure with more debt than equity is usually trouble, but this must be taken in the context of the firm's industry. The banking business effectively borrows money (through your deposits) to lend to others, so by nature banks will have very high debt-to-equity, or debt-to-total-capitalization ratios. Technology companies tend to have more equity (stock) financing, as they would pay higher interest rates for the risk and tend to be able to sell "equity" (stock) at higher prices. Comparative analysis between companies thus comes into play; unfortunately, industry standards, available to professional analysts at a dear price, are hard to come by for free for the individual investor. So beyond comparing a handful of companies, it becomes more of a judgment call.

Active investors should look at total debt and long-term debt (our LCAV example has no long-term debt, which is usually a good thing) and whether debt is increasing. Finally, it is good to examine whether or not the company could easily pay off its debt if it had to—comparing cash balances and cash flows to debt amounts makes sense.

Is the Company Overcapitalized?

Having too much owner's equity—or too many owners—may sound like a good problem to have. Indeed, it is better than the converse, where the business is undercapitalized and burdened with debt. But some companies—notably ones in the high tech sector—have so much capital (shares outstanding) that it's hard to make visible forward progress. On the earnings front, a company like Cisco, which has almost seven *billion* shares outstanding, must earn $70 *million* more just to improve their earnings per share by one cent. Even at their healthy current net profit margin of 19 percent, they must generate almost $370 million in new business just to deliver this one-penny increase.

Microsoft has more than 10 billion shares outstanding. Why did this happen? Numerous stock splits for one; and an extremely strong public perception of these companies, for another. It's hard to find an institution or fund that does not hold one of these companies, particularly Microsoft. That's a good thing—especially if you invested early—but now, the slightest bit of bad news could shake billions of shares out of the institutional tree. Who will buy them? Moreover, at any point in time, there are always plenty of shares available on the market. When there are plenty of shares available—plenty of supply—pure economics suggest little price increase. This has dogged such large caps as Microsoft, GE (10 billion shares), Cisco, Nokia (5 billion), Hewlett-Packard (3 billion), and others.

There are downsides, but value investors often seek companies with relatively few shares outstanding, where demand can truly exceed supply and where management has resisted the temptation to sell overpriced shares and/or split the stock. LCAV has only 14 *million* shares outstanding, and part of its 2004 price strength is almost certainly related to institutions trying to accumulate relatively scarce shares. Companies with fewer than 100 million shares outstanding are usually more attractive, but this is hardly the sole criterion for stock selection. Investors should also seek companies with a track record or strategy of reducing the number of shares outstanding.

Does the Investor Come First?

This is what should be the *true* bottom line (beyond the accounting bottom line) for any investor: Does the interest of the investor come first, and do the actions of the company consistently benefit its investors? Obviously, investors can't know everything going on inside the boardrooms and decision-making sessions in the business, but there are clues to look for.

Dividends

The topic of dividends and whether they are good for investors has been frequently debated. The Bush Administration's 2003 tax changes returned the debate into the spotlight. The changes effectively reduced the tax rate on dividends on stocks held more than one year to make these dividends more attractive. So are they?

The case for dividends is built around the fundamental basis for an equity investment: It should provide regular cash returns to investors. The intrinsic value model suggests that investment is determined by these cash flows—so there must be cash flows, right? The case against dividends: Good companies have better opportunities to invest earnings for better returns than you can get for yourself. They reinvest earnings as retained earnings supposedly capable of achieving 10, 15, or 20 percent returns (which may be true), whereas you can only expect to achieve market returns or slightly more.

The value investing "truth" is somewhere in between. Value investors tend to like *some* cash flow paid as dividends with *some* earnings retained in the business. Good businesses are as a rule worth investing in, and this includes investing some portion of its earned profits (it's better than borrowing the capital, for one thing). But enlightened investors also want clues that management is looking out for them, and what better way to demonstrate this than to pay them something in return for their hard-earned capital? What is sought is a compromise where investors get something and the business gets what it needs. Businesses that retain all earnings as capital, particularly with stated policies of never paying dividends "in the foreseeable future" must go further to gain a value investor's trust.

Share Buybacks

Share buybacks are another way for investor-conscious management teams to give something back to investors. For some companies it's the stated and preferred method (particularly before the Bush Administration dividend tax preference). With share buybacks, the company goes to the open market to buy its own shares for cash, thus retiring them. The result is fewer shares of the same business and fewer slices in the earnings pie, so each remaining shareholder gets more. Higher earnings-per-share results (or should result) in a higher stock price, one way that remaining shareholders get something back from the company.

The Great Option Debate

The option "disease" struck most in the high-tech business, where lean finances and the promise of gain induced companies to reward employee performance with options instead of precious cash. There was no required accounting entry—no expense on the income statement and no cash transaction—to cover these costs. It is essentially a financial freebee, except to the poor shareholder down the road when shares are sold effectively below market price or, worse, when company resources are spent to buy them back. Many financially conservative companies, like Microsoft and others outside the high-tech sector, have decided to expense these options, and some like Hewlett-Packard have had the decision made for them by shareholders in a proxy vote. Imprecise valuation (after all, the real value isn't known until exercise) is the argument against full accounting, but the real issue is impact on earnings. Options, where not expensed explicitly, are disclosed in a financial statement footnote known as "FAS 123." Financial regulators are working to standardize option treatment in the statements, but at the time of this writing it hasn't happened yet.

Some companies state policies for regular share buybacks, while others do it on a decision basis announced with fanfare ("Company XYZ just announced a $1 billion share buyback . . ."). Companies with sustained programs to buy back shares specifically to grow per-share value are the most attractive. You should see decreases in number of shares outstanding in the statements. Here's the "gotcha": Many companies buy back shares just to neutralize the number of options granted to employees. There is no sustainable decrease in the number of shares outstanding; it is simply a transfer of wealth from shareholders to the employees who received the options. If share buybacks are exhibited in the cash flow statement, and outstanding shares stay the same with numerous option grants, you've likely discovered this scenario.

Acquisition Strategy

It happens again and again. Big and often successful businesses hit a growth wall; there simply aren't enough people on this (or any other) planet to sell more products to. So they start acquiring companies, essentially buying "top-line" (revenue) growth. Some of these acquisitions do create shareholder value by expanding into new markets (as many bank mergers have), removing competitors (HP-Compaq), filling gaps in product portfolios (many drug and technology mergers) or achieving economies of scale (again, bank mergers, oil companies). But when it seems like a company is buying others because it has no better way to achieve growth (GE, Cendant)—look out. There is no certain way to judge this; it requires an understanding of the business and the markets operated in. Does the company make a lot of acquisitions? Is there a strategy? Look at what they say—and what they do.

Ratio Analysis

Financial analysts worldwide employ ratio analysis to try to understand businesses through their financial statements. Ratios are just what the name implies: One financial statement item is divided by another, yielding a third figure, the ratio. Ratios help you to understand the business and provide a quick and easy standard for comparison.

Dozens of ratios are used, and some are more important than others. Some are industry specific, but most are universal. For the purpose of this book, ratios can be grouped into four types: *profitability, productivity, financial strength,* and *valuation*.

Profitability Ratios

Profitability ratios take profits or profit drivers and compare them to key figures on the statements; chiefly revenue, assets, and equity. Here are a few, some seen earlier in the initial profitability assessment of the company:

- *Return on Sales* is essentially the profit margin: net profit divided by total sales or revenues.
- *Gross Margin* is (sales *minus* cost of goods sold) divided by sales.
- *Operating Margin* is (sales *minus* cost of goods sold *minus* operating expenses) divided by sales.
- *Return on Assets* is net profit divided by total assets and is a measure of how efficiently assets are used in the business.
- *Return on Equity* is net profit divided by total shareholder's equity; the ultimate measure of investor return, except that accounting equity may not be the truest measure. Still, this measure is used by many as one of the first yardsticks.
- *Return on Invested Capital* is net profit divided by (owner's

equity *plus* long-term debt)—a truer indication of return for *all* who have committed capital, not just owners.

Productivity Ratios

Return on assets is the bottom-line productivity ratio, but many analysts like to take this figure apart to figure out how efficiently the company is using accounts receivable, inventories, fixed assets, and other assets. Unit productivity ratios are also included. These ratios are effective both as "over time" measures and as comparative yardsticks to other similar businesses:

- *Receivables turnover* is sales divided by accounts receivable, thus indicating how much credit a company must extend to gain sales.
- *Average collection period* (or days' sales in receivables) is 360 divided by receivables turnover, and it shows the average number of days that receivables are on the books. This is an indicator of credit extension, customer quality, and the effectiveness of collection efforts. If the collection period is increasing, watch out.
- *Inventory Turnover* is sales divided by total inventory. Efficient companies generate more sales per inventory dollar invested.
- *Fixed Asset Turnover* is sales divided by fixed assets. It shows how well a firm uses fixed assets, although this is subject to distortion through depreciation activity.
- *Total Asset Turnover* is sales divided by total assets. It tests overall asset structure and efficiency, including intangibles.
- *Unit Productivity* measures include sales per employee, sales per square foot, same store sales, average selling price, revenue per customer, customer acquisition cost, and industry-specific measures such as revenue per seat mile used by the airline industry. If you can get them, use them!

Financial Strength Ratios

Financial strength ratios test the financial viability of the company, and they are aimed at judging debt and debt levels. Debt-to-equity and debt-to-total assets ratios measure the size of debt as compared to owner's investment and to the business itself.

Valuation Ratios

The ratios shown so far examine the internal finances of the business. But what about the price of shares? Is the company valued appropriately for those considering a commitment of capital? Valuation ratios bring a new factor into the equation—the *price* of the firm's shares. Many of these ratios—particularly the Price/Earnings, or P/E, ratio, are familiar.

Price/Earnings Ratio. "P/E" is simply the current price of the stock divided by earnings per share for the trailing twelve months. It is sometimes referred to as the "trailing" P/E ratio, while a "forward" P/E ratio compares price to *projected* per-share earnings over the next twelve months. What "should" a P/E be? The answer is complex. Different P/E standards apply to different industries, and P/E is also driven by the returns available on alternative investments, thus will be higher when fixed returns or interest rates are low. The next metric that follows makes more sense of this.

Earnings Yield. "EY" is simply the reciprocal of P/E and represents the effective yield of the investment. A stock with a P/E ratio of 25 has an earnings yield of 4 percent (1/25), and thus can be compared with other investments, including relatively risk-free interest bearing investments. If you're investing in a stock with a P/E of 25, the return should be better than the alternative yields available. But there's another factor to consider: growth.

Price-to-Earnings-to-Growth. The price-to-earnings-to growth, or "PEG" ratio, normalizes P/E ratios to account for growth; that is, a stock with a P/E of 25 and an annual earnings growth rate of

Appraising a Business: A Value Approach 137

25 percent has a PEG of 1, much better than another stock with a P/E of 25 and a more meager earnings growth rate of 5 percent; that PEG is 5. Recalling the earlier discussion of intrinsic value, companies with sustainable growth have higher long-term cash returns and thus higher intrinsic value. Paying 25 times current earnings may be justified with a high projected growth rate. Generally, stocks with a PEG of less than 1 are attractively priced, and ones with a PEG over 3 are overpriced.

Price-to-Cash-Flow. Realizing that cash flow, especially over the long term, may be a better indicator of true business activity, some analysts look at price-to-cash-flow as an alternative to P/E. Some dig further to look at price-to-free-cash-flow, that is, cash flow available after capital investments.

Price-to-Sales. "P/S" is a quick indicator of price acceptability. It is the ratio of price to per-share revenues or sales, sometimes also calculated as "market capitalization" (price of shares times number of shares outstanding) divided by total revenues. As an individual buying a business, you would hesitate to pay three or four times annual sales for a business; ideally this ratio would be one or less. Such is also true for investments, although growth rates and profit margins must be considered.

Price-to-Book. "P/B" is share price divided by the accounting book value, or owner's equity, per share. Unfortunately, as discussed earlier, the book value may not reflect reality, so this measure is relatively less useful for most industries. It does have merit in financial services and similar industries, where most of the assets are cash and securities.

Summing up, ratios are handy ways to gauge the success of a business, and particularly to compare it to other businesses. Ratios help make sense of the financials and the stock price.

All financial analysts, amateur or professional, must avoid the temptation to use ratios and other financial analysis tools without thinking about the underlying numbers. If a company takes a one-time charge for a restructuring or layoff, the P/E will be distorted by the earnings "hit." So it helps to examine the underlying financials, including the company's own discussion, before taking the analysis as gospel. That said, a company that has these "special" occurrences all the time (and some companies do) should be judged accordingly.

Strategic Intangibles

"Strategic intangibles" are a set of business factors creating an environment for successful financial performance. Essentially, they are leading indicators. These factors include markets and market position, operational and supply chain considerations, and management quality. While financial analysis is largely fact-driven, the assessment of intangibles is much more intuitive and subjective. But active investors must consider strategic intangibles, as market, operational, or management weaknesses can predict future short-term and long-term trouble.

Market Presence

Few factors play more strongly into the success of a business today than its market presence and position. Market presence includes position, competitive profile, market share, brand value, and "moats" (competitive barriers). As an investor, you want to understand all of the above, though not at the level of detail of a marketing professional.

Positioning

Positioning refers to the strategic direction of the company in its market, and the role it plays in that market. Positioning can emphasize price, service, image, different channels (as in direct or through retail), and many other elements of what's known as the marketing mix. Dell Computer is not just another computer company—they have taken a strategic position of being the lowest-cost direct supplier of customized PC hardware. Lately they have expanded that position to be the same thing for server hardware, printers, and storage devices. Positioning is not accidental; it is a deliberate and thought-out strategic premise for the business. As an investor, you should be able to understand the business and particularly the intended—and accomplished—position of the company in its marketplace. If you can't figure it out, the company either doesn't have a strategy or doesn't have a very good one. *Focus* is important, too. Companies that are trying to be in two or more places at once—such as Daimler-Chrysler, Hewlett-Packard, or United Airlines—have more trouble achieving success in any of them, as resources are diluted and internal struggles abound.

Competitive Profile

Competitive analysis is a mandatory task for the informed investor. Before investing in a business, it is only rational to figure out how many competitors they are, who they are, how they compete, and how effective they are. Who "owns" what parts of the market? What submarkets, or niches, do they serve? What is their overall market share? What is their share of the submarkets or niches? How do they acquire customers and keep the ones they have? How does the public—and their customer base—*perceive* the company and its products? Is the company getting better or worse in these areas?

As a rational active investor, you need to assess these factors at least at a high level, particularly if considering a long-term investment. This is difficult to do, particularly if you're an industry outsider (which is why investing in industries you're familiar with or work in sometimes is easier). There are few places to get complete summaries of all of the above, but it can be pieced together from Value Line summaries, industry and trade publications, the company's own marketing materials, 10-K reports, and your own "on the ground" assessment.

Brand Value

Few assessments are more subjective than the value of a brand, yet brands can be one of the most valuable assets of the business. Consider Starbucks, Coke, Dell, McDonald's, Bose, and individual brands with a "house of brands," like Tide, Lexus, and Minute Maid. Among many other things, brands convey image, value, and trust to their customers, making them largely willing to pay more for their products and services. Naturally, this leads to greater financial value—profits—and it also provides significant barriers to competitor entry. A good brand has enduring value, which the management team must take care of by keeping quality and image intact and avoiding the temptation to spread the brand into too many unrelated things. Active investors should always evaluate the value of a company's brands, even in business-to-business markets. Each summer, *BusinessWeek* publishes an annual survey of brand "value"—an appraisal of the financial value and change in value of the Top 100 brands in business. This is a must-read for the active investor.

Moats

"Moats" are metaphoric barriers to entry. In free markets, companies achieve sustainable competitive advantage by being the "best" at what they do and by, as much as possible, creating barriers to entry for competitors. Good brands are among the most obvious moats—imagine what it would take to build a better brand than Coke or Pepsi. Moats also include intellectual property (patents) and know-how, strong positions in specific markets or customer segments, and power in the distribution channels or in the supply chain. Wal-Mart has a moat around its business because of its buying power and supplier relationships, which enable it to sell many products cheaper than competitors. Microsoft is probably the ultimate example of a company surrounded by a near-impenetrable moat—the control of the standard PC operating system. True there are others—Apple OS and Linux, but only Linux seems to have an outside chance of penetrating. Meanwhile, Microsoft enjoys massive pricing power, gross margins, and so on.

Pricing Power

Far beyond safety, moats give a business *pricing power*. That is, such competitive barriers give a firm more control over its prices, which can be enormously important to creating shareholder value. Pricing power arises not only from moats, but also more generally from favorable competitive position and supply-demand imbalances. Do oil companies have pricing power? You bet. Insurance companies? Yes, to the extent that even state regulation has had little effect. PC manufacturers? Hardly any. Value-oriented investors look for companies with pricing power in their markets, and shifts in pricing power can often be a target for rotational investments. Recent shifts in the supply and demand for raw materials, brought on largely by growth in China, have suddenly enabled basic material suppliers to gain pricing power.

Supply Chain

Rational investors also look for supply chain strength and control. What do we mean by "supply chain"? Supply chain is the chain of inputs necessary for a company to deliver its product or service, and in an expanded sense it includes the channels through which a company markets its products. The supply chain for auto manufacturers includes such elements as steel and plastics manufacturers, parts makers, tire manufacturers, and it extends down to the dealer network. For retailers, the supply chain is their network of manufacturers, importers, and distributors. For PC manufacturers, it is Microsoft, Intel, and an assortment of smaller parts manufacturers.

Good businesses control or influence their supply chain and business inputs, or are less affected by changes in these inputs. Wal-Mart controls its suppliers, while Sears once did but does less so today. By contrast, airlines have no control over fuel and labor prices, and they are significantly impacted every time the price of fuel rises.

Tying together competitive position, moats, market structure and pricing power, one learns to look for companies with a unique and unassailable position in a supply chain. Again, Microsoft presents a "poster child" example, where almost all PCs sold through a multitude of manufacturers must source Windows from Microsoft. These "hourglass" positions exist elsewhere on a small scale, as with companies that supply certain supplies used in medicine. Simpson Products, an old-line manufacturer supplying almost all metal connectors and "joist hangers" to the construction industry, is another example. It's another way to find sustainable competitive advantage.

Is Management on Your Side?

Entire books are written on management, management style, and quality. Here, the point will be condensed into a few short sentences. Good businesses almost always have good management, especially in the absence of some other systematic monopoly power, or moat. What is "good management"? Here are some things to look for:

- *Results.* A company should have steady and predicable results.
- *Clearly articulated strategy.* It's surprising how rare this is, but a management team that communicates a strategy in clear, understandable terms and sets out to execute it gets favor. Watch for overuse of "buzzwords," or the absence of a strategy altogether. For example, cost cutting is not a strategy—it doesn't deliver direct value to customers, differentiate products in the marketplace, nor is it sustainable—and yet it is often offered as a "strategy" to investors.
- *Ownership of results*—good or bad. Good management teams don't hide bad performance—they disclose it and talk about it openly. They also own up to mistakes and product blunders instead of trying to fight them in court.
- *Transparency.* Management teams that communicate to shareholders and the press have less to hide and are more confident in their own capabilities and their organizations. Arrogant behavior, "invincibility," and childish bashing of competitors is not a substitute for good communication. It is difficult to know what goes on inside the many walls of a company, but sharp investors pick up the subtle clues. That said, financials and marketplace performance are probably more dependable indicators of value; management quality is an added bonus.

The Business Appraisal

This necessarily brief treatment of the value investing premise is designed to arm you with the logic and ability to ferret out value in the business world and stock marketplace. The point is to think strategically about value—you may have to read more to learn the tactics, or details, of value assessment.

Value principles should be put into play in all portions of the active investor's portfolio. The deployment of value principles is obvious for the long-term "cornerstone" portfolio, where steady financials, growth through strong marketplace fundamentals and management, and attractive buy-in prices are all important to achieving better than average market returns. But for shorter-term plays, value becomes a selection tool and a way to narrow down choices. Why? A company with solid fundamentals is at least somewhat shielded from declines. If your timing is off and you buy in at too high a price, the underlying value provides something of a safety net. To put it another way, value fundamentals provide a *margin of safety* and reduce risk in all parts of the active investing portfolio.

In practice, active investors should create a checklist covering financial, marketplace, and management fundamentals. There is no company in the universe that scores "A+" in all areas, and more than likely some of the areas will just be educated guesses. That said, the more that is known and judged rationally, the better off your investment outcomes are likely to be.

Points to Remember

- Look at the financials, and look especially for indicators of success such as free cash flow, increasing profit margins, asset quality, optimal capitalization, and returns to investors. Profitability, productivity, and financial strength ratios can help compare performance over time and compare companies to one another. Valuation ratios can help determine if the "price is right."

Appraising a Business: A Value Approach

- Don't stop with the financials. Marketplace and operational excellence foretell financial performance. Does the company have a clear strategy? Are they executing it successfully? Examine the company's market position and success, including brand value, customer perception, "moats," and pricing power. Evaluate the company the way its customers would. Look for signs that company management is working for you. These fundamentals won't guarantee success, but if you stick with companies that pass these tests, your chances for success will increase in all parts of your active portfolio.

Part IV:

Trading Tools and Techniques for Active Investors

Chapter 10

Playing for the Short Term

Active investors might be described as "value-oriented opportunists." What does this heady phrase mean? Chapters 8 and 9 developed the concept of value investing across all time horizons, long and short. Active investors start with a value-oriented thought process. In this way, investments are viewed as a share of a whole; a stock as a share of a business; and the value of that business is understood and compared to the price paid. This chapter shows how to blend the value thought process with short-term trading techniques in order to capture special short-term market opportunities and turn them into profits.

Markets aren't always right. Short-term distortions in the perception—that is, the market price—of an asset's value happen all the time. These distortions, viewed through a value investor's lens, provide opportunities for short-term gains with relatively minimal risk. Why "minimal risk"? Because the fundamental value of the investment provides a safety net. And what kinds of opportunities? Distortions occur because of market cycles and events, individual company events, and coverage by financial analysts and journalists. There is a lot of market "noise" often obscuring the real value of an investment, and investor uncertainty and emotions not infrequently overtake rational price behavior.

This chapter explores some of the more accepted (or if preferred, less exotic) trading techniques used by active investors to convert these opportunities into gains. Understanding major markets and their inner workings is the first stop on this journey. Next, in Chapter 11, are some of the more accepted and commonly used technical indicators and patterns used to recognize opportunities. Chapter 12 then moves into a more tactical discussion of buying and selling—what kinds of trades to make, and when to sell. Finally, the strategic use of trading tools to manage the active portions of your portfolio is summarized. The objective throughout is to teach you to recognize short-term market opportunities and to capitalize on them, all in a framework of constrained time and personal commitment to the trading process.

It Isn't Day Trading

At the moment you first set eyes on this book, you probably wondered whether "active investing" is "day trading." Day trading, of course, was the late 1990s craze brought on by the availability of rapid-fire, in-out trading to the masses. A steadily rising market made gains relatively easy to capture and it became a profitable enterprise for many.

Day traders seek short-term intra-day profits in the market, committing capital only for the day (usually, for a matter of minutes or even seconds) to capture short-term price fluctuations. At the end of the day, this capital is converted back to cash and removed from the market. Essentially, day traders play in the market as dealers, buying stocks for the very short term in the expectation that a retail investor will come along within moments to buy that security at a higher price. (The operative word can also be "sell"—as day traders play downtrends as well.)

Some traders, known as "scalpers," seek just to capture the retail markup—the difference between the "bid" and "ask" or "offer" prices of the stock—all done alongside real Wall Street dealers and market makers. Scalpers operate in time horizons measured in seconds. Other "momentum" traders try to capture price trends occurring throughout the day, holding the stock for hours as the day's prevailing direction drives it higher or lower. The keys to day trading are fast access to information (news, price behavior, dealer quotes) and fast access to the markets. Like anyone attending any auction market, day traders try to get in line before the rest of the market to get the best buying opportunities and, later on, reap the largest gains.

True day traders, unlike value investors, care little about the companies they trade and still less about their fundamentals. The success and prospects for the company mean nothing—unless the trader is trading off of breaking news bringing more investors to the market. Profits accrue to the "early bird" trader. Some traders follow the behavior of one or a handful of stocks, becoming "experts" on those stocks much as a professional dealer does. Others scan the premarket news for "what is going down today," and trade those stocks accordingly.

Why Did the Gold Rush End?

Day trading is a full-time commitment, as traders are compelled to watch their plays and market events in real-time. Many "pioneer" traders didn't get this—and didn't appreciate how truly mentally and physically demanding this sort of concentration is—and they failed. It still happens today—people respond to juicy advertisements to quit their day jobs, take up trading, and hit the golf course every afternoon. This scenario didn't happen for most; success required real work, and it went on premarket, postmarket, and through the weekend.

This difference between perception and reality combined with fundamental changes in the markets to throw water on the initial day trading boom. Today, day trading is reported to be on the increase, as markets are returning to health and predictability and players learn from their mistakes. The downsizing of trading increments into pennies from eighths eliminated a lot of trading opportunity for scalpers. Real dealers became wiser to traders and developed ways to feint the market to drive them away and cause them to mistime trades, thus recapturing some of their own lost profits.

Day Trading Compared to Active Investing

Like day traders, active investors try to capture short-term opportunistic profits. But that's where the similarity ends. First, the time horizon for active investors is usually longer. Active investors don't watch everything to the minute or second, but instead may check in with the markets a few times a day. This doesn't allow such rapid-fire trading, particularly scalping, as is performed by the full-timer. Most active investors seek the *swing trade*—that is, the market distortion that works itself out in a few days, or maybe a few weeks. Many active swing trades work when the market direction changes, when the impact of a news item dissipates or is replaced by another, or when the investing public returns to the underlying fundamentals and quality of the business.

The second and more essential difference: active investors are concerned about the underlying fundamentals of their investments. Like day traders, active investors may watch a few stocks very closely, but they watch *both* stock price behavior and underlying business prospects—the financial, marketplace, and operational

Playing for the Short Term

fundamentals—of the company. It is through this lens that they spot value and short-term opportunity. As the market "tide" washes out in a downturn, it may wash their stock out too—but the fundamentals suggest that it will come back, sooner or later, when the tide returns. So the active investor, using a value approach, first selects good businesses, then looks for trading opportunities in their stocks. To repeat a core concept, the value approach reduces the downside risk in the trade.

What Is a "Swing Trade"?

In contrast to the rapid-fire "day" trade, a swing trade is a buy action with intent to sell out of the position in a short time frame, ranging from that same day to a few days or a few weeks later, as conditions dictate. Generally, the trader is betting that very short-term market conditions—an oversold condition, or the dissipation of bad market or company news—will eventually work itself out and the stock will bounce back to a target level. Swing trades may be closed out the same day if the desired conditions occur faster than expected, but more often than not, those conditions happen in a few days to at most a week or two. Swing traders usually set a target price to exit their trades. Swing trades can be on the "sell" side, too—selling "short" with intent to buy back a few days later at a lower price. The success of these trades is based more on the perceived difference between current price and fundamental stock value, and less on the day trader's reflex response to market fluctuation.

Just as importantly, the value-oriented trading approach separates the active investor from the painful task of having to time every trade *perfectly*. If a trade is a good idea, it's a good idea for a few pennies more (or less). The active investor doesn't have to stay glued to tiny second-to-second market fluctuations, nor do they have to pay extra for the direct access or one-second trade execution that is all very important to the otherwise-engaged active investor.

Going Against the Grain

The word "contrarian" describes an investing approach and even the core strategy of some investing funds. "Contrarian" investing refers to investing in businesses or industries that are currently out of favor. Opportunistic active investing is essentially contrarian. As the market tide takes stocks in a certain direction, the active investor, by having a better perception of the true value of a stock, trades against that grain. As a stock price diverges farther from its true value, the opportunity to buy or sell profitably grows. The trick is, of course, to understand its true value. Nevertheless, a value appraisal is a good starting point. As will be shown, an understanding of the core value, combined with certain trading patterns and indicators that help reinforce it, provide trading clues for the value investor.

The Way Things Work

As in any other game, it's important to understand the rules before playing, even if you choose not to become an "expert." Similarly, one should understand the inner workings of major trading venues, mainly the NASDAQ and New York Stock Exchange. When one understands the mechanics of the game and play in practice, one can better decipher its outward signals and more effectively execute strategies as a player.

The Big Board

The well-known New York Stock Exchange remains the world's premier trading venue, though that status is increasingly challenged by more computerized trading platforms characterized by NASDAQ. The NYSE is an "auction" market, where all orders come to an auctioneer, or *specialist*, who matches buy and sell orders and executes trades on behalf of the buyers and sellers. Essentially, one human controls all transactions for a particular stock, known in the trade as a *listed* stock. That "human" maintains a list of all active buy and sell orders in the market, and matches them when the price matches. That "human"—usually an employee of a specialist firm—also carries an inventory of their specialized stock.

Exchange rules require the specialist to "keep an orderly market" by placing their own shares—thus their own interest—on the line to avoid major price disruptions. Exchange rules also require specialists to place customer orders ahead of their own shares at a given price; that is, if you choose to sell at $21.50, the specialist must put your order in front of their own desire to sell inventory at that same price.

Orders are routed to the specialist by an electronic system known as "SUPERDOT," which brings orders from your Internet-based trading platform to the specialist almost instantly. If your order is a "limit" order—that is, if it specifies a price—it is placed in queue among all other orders at that price and matched when an order on the other side (someone else's "sell" matched to your "buy") comes in at that price. If it is a "market" order, it is matched against the best price available on the other side. The "best" bid is the *highest* bid available in the market; if you sell at "market" you'll get this best bid price, if the "size," or number of shares, at that price is sufficient. The best "ask" (or "offer") is the *lowest* price at which shares are available, and your market "buy" order will get this price with sufficient size available. An NYSE quote shows the inside, or best bid and ask prices, with the "size" available for each. For example, using General Electric:

GE Bid $30.25 x 500   Ask $30.27 x 3800

Translation: In the market for GE, the specialist has 3800 shares available for you to buy at $30.27, either from customer orders or from his or her own inventory. At the same time, there are orders to buy (or a specialist's own commitment to buy) 500 shares at $30.25. If you enter an order to sell 400 shares at market, you'll get $30.25. If you enter a "limit" order to sell 400 shares at, say, $30.30, it will be entered in the order queue behind the best offer of $30.27. It will only execute when it becomes the "inside," or best, price, and another market order comes in, or if the specialist decides to take the shares at $30.30 for their own inventory. If you enter a "limit" sell at $30.27, and the only other offer is that of the specialist, your order will "cut in line" in front of the specialist and be shown as available.

The "inside" prices and size—$30.25 by 500, $30.27 by 3800—are the only figures available to anyone beyond the specialist. "Outside" orders—which can tell much about underlying strength or weakness of a stock—are visible only to the specialist. NASDAQ, on the other hand, makes these "away from the market" quotes visible, albeit through the usually expensive "Level II" access window. This lack of "transparency" has garnered a great deal of criticism for the NYSE and put the specialist system on the hot seat. Also drawing fire are recent allegations of specialists overtrading their own accounts—that is, manipulating supply and demand by being "in the market" too often for their own profit. Specialist firms are currently being investigated by the SEC. There is a lot of talk about making NYSE practice more like

NASDAQ, and some major U.S. companies have recently underscored that talk by making their shares concurrently available on NASDAQ and the NYSE.

Active investors watch, bid, ask, and size figures, taking clues as they might with the above quote that the market is weak. There are more shares for sale at the inside offer than others want to buy at the inside bid. Still, there is a lot more to keep in mind. There may be large orders away from the inside, and there may be a floor broker with 100,000 shares to sell currently in discussions with the specialist on the exchange floor. Finally, there is an opportunity to buy or sell shares with some certainty at $30.26, since a limit order placed at that level would "front run" other orders in the marketplace. These clues are useful but usually don't provide enough information for the hard-core day trader. But for a value-oriented active trading approach, the NYSE usually works fine.

NASDAQ

As mentioned before, "NASDAQ" is an acronym for the National Association of Securities Dealers Automated Quotations. For each stock, NASDAQ provides what amounts to an electronic quote board accessible to all dealers, or *market makers* in a stock, and in some cases, to individuals. There may be just a handful of dealers for a less active or well known company, while there will be dozens for the more active NASDAQ stocks like Microsoft and Intel. Each registered dealer is required to post a quote on both sides of the market—at least one bid and one offer—though it doesn't have to be at the inside price or anywhere close. Thus a dealer looking to acquire shares posts aggressive, or high, bids, while a dealer looking to unload shares places low offers.

Like dealers for antiques or any other collectible, and unlike

NYSE specialists (at least in theory), dealers trade primarily for their own accounts. Market makers are individuals, but they work for firms, usually large investment banks or wholesale trading firms choosing to make a market in a stock. Individual market makers are trying to bring profits to the firm by buying low and selling high. Market makers will also trade for specific clients—usually large clients and funds—placing orders into the market on their behalf more or less on consignment, but more of the market maker's activity is related to simply buying and selling out of their firm's inventory.

Sizing Up the Differences

Among the important differences between the NYSE and NASDAQ approach: (1) NYSE has only one "dealer," the specialist, who usually acts as an auctioneer but may also act as a dealer trading for his or her own account, while NASDAQ has many dealers for a stock; (2) NYSE bid/offer prices represent actual orders, while on NASDAQ they are only quotes.

As an investor, your order is routed to market and filled by a dealer. If it is a market order, it usually goes to the first "inside" quote automatically; if it is a "limit" order, the dealers will see it and act on it according to their own interests. A system called "SOES"—Small Order Execution System—automatically routes market orders to a dealer on the inside and executes them, requiring no human involvement. SOES orders are fast and reliable, but they are only for orders of 1000 shares or fewer. High-performance trading platforms allow individual traders to select specific dealers to trade with and to place orders directly onto the order board, but this capability usually isn't necessary for the active investor.

Playing for the Short Term

Dealer activity on NASDAQ is represented as quotes only—they aren't specific orders. Quotes show a dealer code (for example, "MLCO" for Merrill Lynch's investment banking arm or "NITE" for wholesaler Knight Trading) and the number of shares available (size) at a price. A quote display (and Level II display) for Microsoft might look like this:

MSFT

	Bid			Ask	
MLCO	200	26.40	JPMS	5000	26.41
MASH	800	26.40	ISLD	400	26.42
ISLD	500	26.39	DEAN	900	26.42
SBSC	200	26.39	ARCH	200	26.44
JPMS	300	26.38	MASH	600	26.45

This is only the very top of the quote list; a Microsoft board will go deep into the hundreds of individual quotes (with Level II access, you can scroll through the entire list). The best bid, posted by MLCO, or Merrill Lynch, is $26.40 by 200 shares, while the lowest offer is made by J.P. Morgan Securities, or JPMS, and is $26.41 by 5000 shares. That price level, $26.40 bid by $26.41 ask, is the "inside" quote available for most electronic "Level I" quotes, like what you see on Yahoo!Finance. As required by NASDAQ, there is at least one MLCO quote on the offer, but it may be at any price level away from the market. These quotes may stay around all day or be replaced in rapid-fire sequence as market conditions or dealer inventories change.

The quote board shown indicates MLCO as a buyer (they are on the inside with the bid but off on the ask) and JPMS as a fairly heavy seller. Perhaps their own analysts have soured on the stock; perhaps they are selling for a large client, or perhaps they are unloading excess inventory or inventory acquired at a lower price. As an active *trader*, you don't know, but you can get clues from watching the behavior of the big players (known colloquially as the "ax" on any given day they are active).

Active *investors* (as opposed to active traders) don't necessarily need to follow the minute-to-minute behavior of these dealers, but it's good to know the dynamics of underlying market activity. By looking at the Level II screen, or Yahoo!Finance "Real-time ECN" quotes, some clues may emerge as to where a stock is going.

Which Is Better—NYSE or NASDAQ?

The "Which market system is best?" debate goes on. Clearly, NASDAQ offers a better system for the real-time day trader. Market transparency, defined as access to the entire quote board at and away from the inside market, gives these traders a clear view of where the puck is going for a stock, though the picture can change in seconds. The multiplicity of dealers can serve to keep things honest; one dealer can't so easily manipulate a price by withdrawing or manipulating quotes, because some other dealer (or an individual through an ECN) will fill the void and set the market straight. With "thinly traded" (low volume, few dealers) situations, some manipulation may occur through dealers trading back and forth with each other to drive prices up or down.

NYSE specialists, on the other hand, are chartered with the responsibility to keep orderly markets by using their own inventory, if necessary. There is no corresponding force or requirement on NASDAQ. On the other hand, whether NYSE specialists actually do give up their own interests to keep orderly markets has come into question, and a market controlled by one player can be bad. For active investing purposes, both venues are adequate, but the evolution of these markets and their rules bears watching.

ECN—The Wave of the Future?

"ECN" is shorthand for Electronic Communications Network, a relatively new and increasingly consumer-oriented electronic marketplace for trading stocks. An ECN is an electronic quote board allowing individuals—and institutions—to trade shares with each other without going through a dealer. Investors can post quotes (size and price) almost as if they were bidding and offering shares on eBay; an investor accepting their quote simply picks it off the board. Originally, ECNs served the needs of institutions seeking to trade with each other "after hours." But the electronic trading revolution has turned other networks into electronic trading venues for active traders everywhere. These traders can get the best price without going to market or can push their orders into NASDAQ directly through these venues. ECNs are capturing increasing market share, and the visibility of ECN quotes gives an idea of "away from the market" supply and demand, showing where the market is going without Level II access to dealer quotes. See Yahoo!Finance "Real-time/ECN" for ECN quotes for a stock.

Chapter 11

Signs of Opportunity

With this groundwork of fundamental value and market operations, how do you, in your daily "active" practice, recognize and act on short-term opportunities? There is no sure-fire method or process, no foolproof way, just like there is no "perfect" best place to live. If there were, everybody would flock to it, and it wouldn't be the best place to live anymore. Similarly if there was a "perfect" trading technique it wouldn't work, because everybody would start to use it and there would be no one to take the other side of the trade. So, to start with, you must have realistic expectations and be willing to deal with failure, learn from mistakes, and accept change.

Yet, as enlightened participants, active investors learn to look for certain market events and patterns that *indicate* opportunity, even if they don't guarantee it. Many professional traders use deep statistical analysis of charts and statistical indicators to time their trades. Active investors don't have the time, nor the bandwidth, to examine such minute details. Instead, they are looking for more high-level patterns and indicators to make their choices. These indications are thrown into the pot with other factors, such as company fundamentals, to arrive at trading decisions. Under no circumstance do active investors "automatically" react to any set of criteria; each decision is a "soup" of weighed pros and cons, or upside and downside risks, to which the current events or patterns add important ingredients. Like any good cook, the active investor learns to recognize which ingredients work best to achieve their own set of desired results.

Events: Scheduled and Unscheduled

Market events and individual company events come in all shapes and sizes. Obviously, the unscheduled news event, particularly unwelcome geopolitical or economic news, can hardly be anticipated. And while some developments, like Middle East tensions, can have cause-and-effect chains that can be easily linked to the performance of individual companies (like energy companies, for example), it is hard to know on a day-to-day basis what will occur where. Such events, like interest rate changes, are best considered as parts of cyclical events or longer-term phenomena. As such, an active investor might capitalize on them in the rotational portfolio, using sector-oriented investments, but the connection between world events and individual stocks is most likely too tenuous and fleeting to trade on actively.

Instead, there are two types of news events, occurring at a company level, that do often provide trading opportunities: earnings announcements and events at "peer" companies—companies in the same industry.

The Earnings Announcement Play

It happens all the time—Company XYZ stock rises to a crescendo close at the end of trading before a quarterly earnings announcement, then "gaps down"—opens far lower than the previous close—at the opening of the following trading session, because, "Earnings were great, but didn't meet some analysts' expectations." This pattern occurs repeatedly. Anxious investors bid up the price in anticipation of a pleasant earnings surprise, and sellers "short" on the stock cover positions just in case it really happens. All of this leads to a price buildup before the announcement. Unless profits, revenues, and everything else—profit margins, unit productivity, balance sheet items, and cash flow—are perfect, the inevitable drop occurs. Like other patterns, this can't be guaranteed, but it happens a lot.

How does the active investor capitalize on the Earnings Announcement ("EA") phenomenon? Here are three ways:

1. Buy a week or so before the "EA," ride the crescendo, and sell near the market close before the announcement. The risk: The company may "preannounce" poor performance, thus driving the stock down before the scheduled announcement.

2. If the stock is already owned, sell as outlined above, or sell covered call options against the stock, thus generating short-term income. (Covered call options are discussed in Chapter 14.) Covered call options preserve ownership in the stock, which may have tax advantages. The downside risk of a truly positive EA is mitigated by the fact you still own the stock and will sell at a profit despite losing on the option play.

3. Use the fallout as a buying opportunity. If you're thinking about picking up the stock anyway, a post-EA drop is usually a good time to do it. Read the EA first, though, to convince yourself that fundamentals are still intact.

Where do you find out about EAs? Most financial portals, including Yahoo!Finance, provide details on upcoming earnings announcements each month.

The Peer Pressure Play

Closely related to the EA play, active investors can occasionally find opportunities to trade followed companies when another company in the industry "blows up," sending shock waves across the sector. The more drastic examples arise from bankruptcies, where a "belly-up" in a key sector, like banking, airlines, or telecom, upsets the entire apple cart. True, it is imperative to recognize the factors that created the bankruptcy, and in the case of steel and airlines, the problems at one company are likely to be problems at another. But in many other cases the situation is neutral or even beneficial to your company, the emerging survivor.

IPOs—An Offer You Can Refuse

One market event *not* advisable to follow is the initial public offering, or IPO. IPOs were a favorite day-trading play in the late 1990s, and indeed a lot could be made by "flipping" these stocks to the onrushing herd of buyers. IPOs are all too often for companies not proven in business or in their marketplace, and their shares are even less proven in stock markets. It is hard to develop a solid rationale for IPO companies; there is seldom a sustained performance or a track record. It is simply too risky a game for the rational investor.

More common—and less risky—is the peer play after an earnings announcement or some other announcement concerning market share, lawsuits, management changes, and so forth. An EA-related drop in Intel stock will almost certainly affect Advanced Micro Devices (AMD) stock, but does it really affect AMD itself? If the "blow up" is based on revenues, could it be

Signs of Opportunity

that AMD, the arch-competitor, actually will benefit? Patient investors think through the reasons that their peer stock is moving "in sympathy." If the underlying business basis and rationale supporting their company is still intact, these events can produce a buying opportunity. This is part of the reason active investors watch industries, not just individual stocks.

Do "Insiders" Really Know More?

Recent legislation, including the SEC's "FD," or Full Disclosure, rule, have attempted to close the gap between those "insiders" who know what's going on in a company and the investing public. While these rules have helped, today's market behavior still reflects a knowledgeable base of traders who know more than the general public. Companies do business with other companies, and, through those business relationships, learn a lot. The "gossip line" also works. If in doubt, just look at the price behavior of key companies before acquisition announcements. The playing field may be a little easier to stand up on, but it still isn't completely level.

Patterns of Success

Markets are nothing more than a collection of interested parties who have shares or want shares—and who have differing opinions about the future price prospects of a stock. It is the collective behavior of those markets that you see in the form of prices and price changes. That collective behavior can be interesting and indicative to analyze over a period of time, for the past may predict the future. While long-term investors care little about the short-term behaviors of the market, active investors looking for short-term opportunities often tune in to try to decipher this collective behavior to their benefit.

The advent of easy-to-use charting tools turns the figurative thousand words—or in this case, datapoints—into a picture. This picture reflects the collective behavior of the market.

What does the active investor look for? Collective behavior is to a large extent random, but it also reflects the behavior, and more subtly, the attitudes of key players in the market. Big traders—investment banks, mutual funds, pension funds—really do drive markets, and they too look for indicators. When big traders see indicators they are often spurred into action, often in a semi-automated fashion ("program trading" is one manifestation). Active investors also look for *bias*—certain signs that key players are leaning one way or another with a stock. Active investors realize that market fluctuations are not necessarily random and reflect a collective behavior among critical buyers and sellers that something may indeed be good or bad about a company. Bias may serve only to confirm an active investor's own appraisal of a company—but it may also help time entry or exit from a stock.

Technical Plays

Although there are myriad observable trading patterns and statistical signals for the purposes of this book and the active investing mentality, we are only going to examine the most popular and easily discerned ones. Bear in mind that the very ease of discerning these signals makes it likely that more people see the same thing you do. That can be good, so long as the masses act in predictable ways to the signal. That doesn't always happen, and it may happen differently with different stocks, which all have different sets of market players. The prudent active investor studies these patterns in a stock over time before going into action.

Relative Strength

Active investors look for signs of short-term and long-term positive (or negative) bias in the collective market. One sign of this is "relative strength"—that is, the strength of an individual stock price performance in respect to its peers, and with respect to the market as a whole. Stocks that don't seem to drop when the Dow is down 130 points in a day—and especially if the sector is showing a big down day—send little flags that something may be right with the company. These signals can be looked at on a short-term, intra-day basis or over the longer term. Although the comparison is often easily "eyeballed," Yahoo!Finance charting and technical analysis tools allow you to compare a stock with any other stock (or sector fund) or with broader market indicators. *Investor's Business Daily* also exhibits relative strength on a percentile scale. "RS" by itself is far from a perfect indicator, but this bias indicator can confirm your own assessment of a stock.

Daily Strength

"Daily strength" is related to "relative strength." Indications that "smart" insiders are buying (or selling) are important. When price "upticks" (changes upward) occur on large volume it is a sign of institutional buying. When this behavior is consistent over a few days, it is a strong positive signal of bias (and conversely, downticks with volume show negative bias). The active investor keeps track using Yahoo!Finance daily and 5-day charts with volume shown along the bottom.

When looking at a trading day, it is often said that "Morning is amateur hour, late afternoon is for the professionals." There is usually a quiet lull in between, while professional traders, often acting on behalf of large funds or institutional investors, wait to decide when to enter (or exit). The active investor thus looks at price activity at the beginning and especially at the end of the day. As in horse racing, fast finishers often win—stocks with a strong upsurge near the close reflect positive bias. Many investors like to see a modestly "V" shaped pattern through the day—a surge in buying at the open confirmed by a surge in buying at the close, with a relatively unimportant midday lull. Successive "V"s indicate professionally driven strength, where upside-down "V"s and especially weak closes indicate weakness.

Moving Averages

Much is made in the trading community of moving averages and the signals they send. Moving averages are simply arithmetic or exponentially weighted averages of the prices of a stock for the previous X number of days. Don't get scared by the term "exponentially weighted"; put simply, this approach "weighs"— gives more value—to the days' prices that occurred most recently. Arithmetic averages, on the other hand, weigh each day's closing price equally. The "exponential" crowd maintains —with some merit—that recent prices are more indicative of future performance.

Yahoo!Finance technical analysis (*finance.yahoo.com*, enter a symbol, and click on "technical analysis") allows for a chart with 5, 10, 20, 50, 100, and 200-day "Moving Avg" lines added to the actual price line of a stock. These arithmetic averages do just as they say—averaging the last 5, 10, 20 . . . 200 days of price behavior. Obviously, the 5-day is more reactive to recent performance than the 200-day, which stays more "smooth" and consistent over time. Thus, changes in the 5-day average reflect more volatility and response to specific market and stock events, while 200-day changes reflect a more fundamental change in direction. Exponential, or "EMA" (Exponential Moving Average) lines weigh more recent events more heavily regardless of

Signs of Opportunity

the time frame of the average, and are preferred by many more sophisticated investors.

What do investors look for? Many look for crossovers—that is, where the actual price line of a stock crosses its moving average. Such crossovers are considered as "buy" or "sell" signals, depending on direction. A crossover to the upside is considered a buy signal, while a crossover to the downside is considered a sell. Underlying this theory are two concepts. First, a stock's crossing of its MA is considered a major change in direction; that is, a fundamental shift in its current price behavior vis-à-vis previously established behavior. Perhaps more realistic is the second: Professional traders, who must keep track of many things at once, rely on computer-generated buy or "watch" signals. These signals pick up this crossing of the average and may become the "barking dog" that brings the trader to focus on the stock and take action.

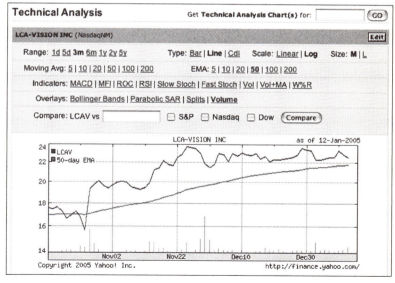

Figure 11.1: LCA Vision 50-Day
Exponential Moving Average—3 months

Figure 11.1 shows an example from Yahoo!Finance technical analysis of a 50-day EMA on LCA Vision stock over a three-month period in early 2004. The negative crossing at the end of February might be looked at as a sell signal; in fact, the stock declined another 10 percent from that level. Similarly, the late March positive crossover signaled strength leading to an almost 40 percent increase at one point. Active investors avoid automatic trades but use such indicators ("barking dogs") announcing opportunity.

Trading Ranges

Trading ranges are what they sound like—a range *within which* a stock typically fluctuates randomly. Without fundamental news or strong external currents, stocks, and particularly widely held "large cap" stocks tend to get stuck in ranges. They will "sawtooth," that is, bounce up and down around an average; when they reach an upper barrier, the investing public (and professional traders) consider them overvalued and sell; likewise, when they reach the bottom of the range, investors tend to step in. Technicians sometimes call these boundaries "support" and "resistance" levels, although these terms are often applied to price levels defined by more sophisticated statistical modeling.

Trading ranges are often easy to discern simply by "eyeballing" a chart, which is part of what makes them attractive to the average investor. See **Figure 11.2** for an example of a growth-value play, CarMax, Inc.

Signs of Opportunity

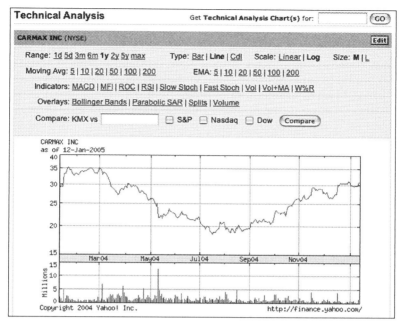

Figure 11.2: CarMax Trading Ranges—1 year

Figure 11.2 shows a stock trading in a 30 to 35 range for a lengthy nine-month period from July 2003 through March 2004. With a few exceptional "pops" over 35 in Fall 2003, the stock bounced between 30 and 35 consistently. Only the market-driven fear of increased interest rates and lower consumer confidence knocked the stock out of its range at the end. Traders could have done well by buying at 30, selling (or selling call options) at 35.

Trading ranges do tend to change; usually setting themselves up after a short up or down move into another trading range. Trading range plays work better when there's no specific news—like interest rate changes—driving major changes in the market. They also work better for stocks with larger capitalization, where more people are watching and it takes a stronger force to knock them out of the range.

Signs of Change in Trading Ranges

Sharp-eyed traders try to pick up clues that a stock is about to move to a new trading range. Such a prognosis might cause an investor *not* to sell, for instance, when the stock hits the top of its range. One obvious sign is a specific news event, which can naturally cause the market to change its perception of the stock's value. Another, more subtle, message apparent in the charts is when the stock fails to touch both ends of the range consistently. A stock that hits the high end, but sets consistently higher "lows," may be ready to "break out" into another higher range. Of course, the reverse is also true.

Some stocks, particularly with smaller capitalization, may exhibit trading range behavior contrary to intuitive logic—that is, the idea that when a company "breaks out" of a trading range that this is a buy or sell signal. A company breaking through the high end of the range is a buy, "resistance" is "taken out" and it will move higher. Naturally, it works the other way on the downside. This can be especially true with thinly capitalized stocks, like LCA Vision. Instead of more shares becoming readily available, which happens on "large cap" stocks, as it reaches its resistance level, the upside signal sets people—notably dealers—into a scramble when there aren't enough shares available to satisfy demand when an upside signal occurs. Similarly, a relative flood of shares becomes available (often from dealers) when a stock is perceived as "weak" at the support level. This phenomenon is common in more volatile (especially technology) shares. The example of LCA Vision (**Figure 11.3**) appears to behave this way. As shown, when LCAV broke out of the 15–20 range, it went higher; and did so again, breaking out of the 20–25 range.

Signs of Opportunity 175

Figure 11.3: LCA Vision Trading Ranges—6 months

You may have noticed the round figures of 15 to 20, 20 to 25. This is no coincidence: Support and resistance levels, and thus trading ranges, are not only psychological but tend to match price targets set by professional traders, either mentally or with automated trading tools. Whether it's a five-dollar increment, or something larger or smaller, it varies by stock, but you'll seldom observe a trading range falling between $26.77 and $29.43. Finally, the time horizon for trading ranges varies, usually according to the volatility of the stock and its underlying industry. Many traders use intra-day trading ranges to time trades. Regardless, the prudent active investor studies trading range behavior over a period of time before committing capital.

Bollinger Bands

The heady-sounding "Bollinger band" is really a statistically determined trading range, one simultaneously more precise and more responsive to changing conditions. Simply, Bollinger bands define a trading range based on previous fluctuations, or "standard deviation," of a stock's price. That is, based on a statistical analysis of price fluctuations, Bollinger bands define a range outside of which the stock is not likely to move except under extraordinary circumstances. Thus, a stock with large fluctuations will have a wider trading range than one that does not. This is one key to understanding Bollinger bands; the other is to realize that as fluctuations increase or decrease, the size of the trading range grows or shrinks accordingly.

Bollinger bands are readily available on Yahoo!Finance technical analysis, and on many other charting platforms:

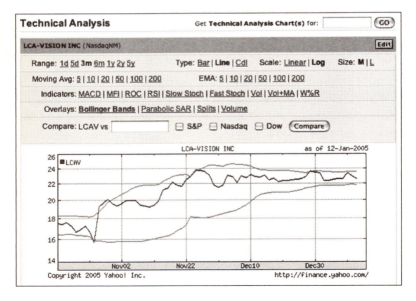

Figure 11.4: LCA Vision Bollinger bands

Signs of Opportunity

This chart shows the behavior of the bands as price barriers. When the price touches the band it is an alert to consider buying or selling, or at least to watch it very closely. Buying at a "low" touch and selling at a "high" touch can work, but there is often an increase in volatility signifying a forthcoming price move; it becomes apparent with the movement of the band. Thus it isn't an automatic buy or sell.

Candlestick Charts

Though originated in ancient Japan to chart the movement of basic foodstuff prices, candlestick charts have grown in popularity among investors as a way to quickly grasp trading ranges and bias all in one picture. Each trading day is represented by a candle. The thin "wick" through it shows the full high-low range from that day, while the thicker "candle" depicts the difference—and direction of movement—between the open and closing prices. Taken together, and especially over a period of time, the size and shape of candles has meaning, although interpretation is subjective (and is the subject of many books).

The "hollow" candles show a positive difference between opening and closing prices, while a dark solid shows a negative difference—for example, the stock price failed through the day. A long hollow indicates upward bias, as the stock closes strong through the day. A short hollow at the top of a long wick, called a "hammer" by candlestick technicians, equates with the "V" pattern outlined earlier and is a strong signal, particularly at the end of a downturn. A "star"—created by an opening and closing at the same price with higher and lower intra-day prices, indicates indecision and can signal a top if after a series of "up" days. A long series of hollows shows strength and upward bias while a long series of solids indicates weakness.

Figure 11.5 shows a candlestick chart for LCA Vision:

178 ACTIVE INVESTING

Figure 11.5: LCA Vision Candlestick chart

Statistical Signals

Statisticians and "quants"—statistical market gurus—have written hundreds of books (and still hundreds more papers) applying some new statistical technique to the analysis and interpretation of "time-series" stock price behavior. Statistics as a science seeks to find and describe a pattern among seemingly random events, and can in fact interpret a lot from apparently unrelated data. Statistical forecasting models prevail in marketing and manufacturing environments, and so long as those using them understand their strengths and weaknesses, they can be quite useful. The same goes for the statistical investor, but all investors must keep in mind that the practice of statistics uses the past to describe the future; like driving a car through the rearview mirror.

The most popular statistical indicators attempt to quantify bias—that is, to measure how much a series of events is correlated

Signs of Opportunity

in a certain direction as opposed to being entirely random. The "MACD"—Moving Average Convergence Divergence—indicator measures the difference between short- and long-term moving averages. When *that difference* changes materially, and particularly when it changes *direction*, that's considered a signal that something fundamental has changed with the price behavior of the stock, and is used as a buy or sell signal.

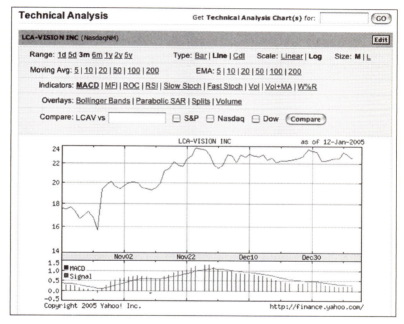

Figure 11.6: LCA Vision–MACD indicator

In the LCA Vision example, a sell signal was sent about February 23, when the MACD "signal" line went negative. In early April a buy signal was sent when the line once again crossed the zero line.

Like most indicators, MACD fits some stocks better than others; you can decide whether this chart is any more or less useful than others. Other statistical indicators include *stochastics*, which take a more direct look at the bias of sequential data points in one direction or another, and the "RSI"—Relative Strength Index—which does much the same thing. For the most part, these tools are designed for more full-time traders who really understand and use them to automate the signaling of trades. Computer programs monitor these signals closely and send alerts to active traders when certain conditions are met. However, as you'll hear and read about these terms some familiarity is valuable for the active investor.

Chapter 12

Buying and Selling

Execution is the next stop on the trading journey. This term refers to the tactics for buying and selling stocks once they are chosen as trading opportunities. Buying and selling tactics don't much affect good long-term cornerstone value plays or most rotational investments, but bad buy/sell tactics *will* undermine the success of a good trading pick. That said, good buy/sell techniques *won't* make up for a bad trading pick.

Fortunately, the markets moved away long ago from an "order is an order" mentality and provided tools for individual investors to control the price of what they buy and sell. Such tools give individual investors the ability to set their prices in the market and—more importantly—the ability to carry out trading strategies and programs without watching the minute-by-minute pulse of the market. The active investor can set his or her own criteria or "rule" for a daily stock trade and go off to do other things: If the conditions consistent with that rule occur, the order is executed automatically. The following sections give an overview of the effective use of market and limit orders, which should help active investors avoid overuse of some of these tools. Also addressed is the all-important topic of when and how to sell as well as sell strategies and sell *discipline*.

Market Orders

As explained earlier, a market order is simply an order to buy or sell at whatever the current market price is. The lack of a specified price makes the order much faster and easier to execute; it can be matched immediately to whatever shares are available at the offer price (for a buy order) or at the bid price (for a sell order). The obvious disadvantage of market orders is the lack of price control: The investor gets whatever the market has to offer at the instant it is executed.

Limit Orders

Limit orders, on the other hand, specify a price, really an "at" price. A buy limit order for 100 shares of GE at $29.80 says "I will buy 100 shares of GE at $29.80 and not a penny more." Similarly, a sell limit order for 100 GE at $30.20 says "I will sell 100 shares at $30.20 and not a penny less." If those prices are never reached for the size specified, the order is never executed, period. Such orders can be set up as "day" orders—that is, they are in force only for the trading day, or as "GTC" (Good Till Canceled)—thus, they stay in force, theoretically forever (different brokers have different rules on this). Most traders use the "day" order, as things can change too much over the "GTC" period. The "buy limit" order is set up to specify your preferred entry price (or price to "cover" a short sale), while the "sell limit" order specifies your target price to sell. The buy limit is effectively a bid in the market, while a sell limit is an "offer" or "ask," and either way, through your broker, they go into the NYSE order queue or NASDAQ quote queue as such. Limit prices set on these orders can be changed indefinitely once placed, and of course, they can be canceled altogether prior to execution.

Buying and Selling

The oft-used strategy of swing-trading the trading range gives a good example of the use of limit orders. The first step is to set up a buy limit order at the low end of the trading range. If that price is "hit" and the order executes (and perhaps you are notified through an e-mail alert) you can turn around and place a sell limit order at a higher price, perhaps the high end of the trading range, and try to capture that day's trading range. The buy limit order should be placed as a "day" order as "GTC" incurs some event risk—risk that the fortunes of a company may change thus making even the lower price too high. The sell limit order, on the other hand, may be placed as a "GTC," capturing your target profit whenever the high end of the trading range is hit.

Stop Orders

A *stop order* is similar to a limit order in that a price is specified; however, when the target price is hit, rather than an automatic execution, the order becomes a market order. The chief use of stop orders is to make orders "active" only when the target price is hit. The best example is the so-called "stop-loss" order. Stop-loss orders, sometimes called *trailing stops*, allow an investor to "bail out" of a stock if it declines to a certain level, providing some downside risk protection. If that investor specified the price as a sell limit, it would be an active order and execute right away, thus making the protection level a self-fulfilling prophecy. The "stop" order keeps the order off the market until the price is met.

As an example, suppose the GE investor bought shares at $30.00 and wanted to set up downside protection at $29.50, in case the market turned dramatically lower or some breaking news event undermined the stock. If they entered a sell limit order at that price, it would execute immediately because the specified price is lower than market; that is, someone on the other side of the trade would immediately absorb the offered shares because the price is below market. Using the stop-loss, on the other hand, renders the order inactive until the "last trade" price is $29.50, so it would only execute when that level is hit. One problem with these orders: they only become active as "market" orders—in a rapid decline the investor might only get $29.40 or less—whatever the market will bear—when they become active. The $29.50 stop price only guarantees the activation of the order, but not the execution at the specified price.

The 10 Percent Sell Rule—Is It a Good Idea?

Investing strategists—and many investing books—promote the idea of selling any stock that declines 10 percent. Why? A 10 percent decline connotes a bad investment idea or decision, and a stock that declines 10 percent is likely to decline further. (Whether such a rule is valid for a value-oriented investor who understands the businesses he invests in is questionable.) Many of these same sources promote the idea of using stop-loss orders behind their investments. Here's the problem, particularly with NASDAQ stocks—dealers can shake the trees to find these stops and take them out, essentially as a source of cheap shares. If they can manipulate the price downward, particularly by trading with each other, they can activate these "trailing stops," sop up the shares, and enjoy the march northward. Investors using sell stops just a little too often might find their sell prices to be the low of the day.

Market Orders *Are* Okay

Serious trading strategists—and their books—go on and on about how one should *never* use market orders; their use subjects investors to the whims of the marketplace dealer markups—

meaning the investor will *never* get the best price. There may be some truth to this argument; for one thing, the investor will always pay the markup through the "offer" price. Markets move quickly, and the stock may move away from the target price as the investor places an order, reducing the effectiveness of the trade. On the other hand, the use of limit orders may cause you to miss the trade altogether—sometimes over a matter of a few pennies per share. Every investor has experienced missing out on a buck-per-share gain because the market didn't quite come down to his or her limit. Limit orders are very useful for certain types of trades, particularly where you can't watch the market actively on a particular day. But if you're trying to capture fifty cents or a buck on a swing trade, don't hold out for a few cents on the limit—if the stock is currently trading about where you want it, just push the "market" button and go for it. If the trade was a good idea in the first place, a few cents won't matter so much, and you'll know right away that you got the shares. The serious day trader cares about the pennies, but the active investor usually doesn't.

The Hardest Part—When to Sell

Most investors and traders alike agree that selling is the hardest part. Catch a winner and the temptation is to let it ride and bask in the glory. Catch a loser and the temptation is to overextend hope—"it certainly will come back; it *has* to." Either way, investors have a tendency to "marry" their stocks, and only consider divorce in the most dire circumstances. These feelings are reinforced when they indeed do sell an investment too soon.

Articles and books on sell rules abound—the 10 percent sell rule explained above is an example. Active investors don't like rules; they tend to consider each case on its merits and rationale. So the following might be considered sell "paradigms" or philosophies:

1. *Sell when there is something better to buy.* Active investors should always look for the best place to deploy their capital. Regardless of the portfolio—foundational, rotational, or opportunistic—the question should always be "Is there something better?" A stock may not have performed according to expectations, but if there's nothing better and the fundamental rationale is still valid, why sell it? Too many investors succumb to the 10 percent rule when in fact, there is no place better to put their money. So they lose 10 percent again on something else!

2. *Sell when fundamentals change.* This may seem obvious and somewhat related to Rule #1, but if a company loses its way it should be sold. A reversal in financial or marketplace performance, if judged likely to be sustained, signals that its time to sell. Declining market share, poorly received products, declining profit margins, a reversal in cash flow, a downside earnings surprise—these and many others can justify a sell, now better than later.

3. *Sell when targets are met.* Again, regardless of the portfolio, when you invest you should have some idea of what you expect from that investment. Make a buck on a swing trade, make 20 percent on a rotational investment, double your money on a long-term foundational investment—hitting such targets signals that it's time to at least evaluate a sale. Some investors sleep better if they *just do it*, and the disciplined "just do it" isn't a bad strategy. A smaller-than-possible profit is always better than a loss, and the active investor should avoid the temptation to hit "home runs." Defining "single" and "double" performance (50 cents, one-dollar gain, for example) as the trade is entered is an idea that works for many.

Selling Short

To sell short is to bet on a decline in the price of a stock. Investors borrow shares from their broker (at an interest rate equivalent to the margin rate) and sell them, hoping to *cover,* or buy them back, at a lower price. Selling short is almost universally a short-term opportunistic strategy brought on by short-term overvaluation distortions in the stock market. Short selling carries unlimited risk, for a stock price can rise indefinitely, whereas a buyer only incurs the risk to zero, so short sellers must have an even temperament, strong discipline, and be able to watch closely. Still, many investors have earned returns selling short, and in the active investor's strategy, selling short as a hedge against the foundation portfolio makes some sense. If they lose on opportunistic short sales, at least some gains may accrue the foundation portfolio. Short selling can only be done on an uptick—that is, on an upward price change, so the short seller must bet on a reversal of direction. Short selling is something to learn by doing, with small experiments in the beginning.

Doubling Down

If an active investor is truly confident in his businesses, the doubling strategy works. Put simply, you invest, and if the price declines, invest more, thus averaging down the entry price. It is an active form of the popular dollar cost averaging strategy. The caveat: Don't do this if there is a fundamental flaw in the investment. The second investment should be considered on its own merits, not just because you already have money committed. There is a big difference between a successful double-down and throwing good money after bad.

Half Selling

Selling half of an investment (or some other portion) when a price target is reached is a good sell discipline designed to capture at least some gain. If the stock continues to rise, you still have something on the table; if it falls, you can buy back in at a lower price, thus capturing a profit. Essentially, it provides protection against excessive greed. Price targets can be set for a half-sale and higher for the other half. Again, a half-sell must be considered on its merits at the time—should you sell all instead of half?

Active Trading for Active Investors, in Practice

Active investors need to carefully consider how active they want to be, and how much they want to commit to the "active," or opportunistic, part of their practice. It depends on the resources and time you have available, and your tolerance for risk. Many active investors set aside 10 or 20 percent of their portfolios and manage them actively, at first with a few small "toe-dips," then with a more complete commitment to certain trading strategies.

Active investors approach everything with rationale, and measuring results is the only way to confirm rationale. Moreover, they learn from their results regardless of the portfolio being evaluated. As an active investor, you should always keep active track of your investments and what they produced, and if they didn't produce, why.

A degree of discipline is important for any investor; it is never a good idea to throw around hard-earned money without at least a degree of care. However, discipline is even more important for active investors. The basis for active investing is informed rationale, so part of the discipline is doing the "due diligence"—research and evaluation—of investments. Buying and especially selling requires discipline, not only to avoid losses but also to avoid excessive greed—the worst enemy of *any* investor. While hard-and-fast execution rules can be counterproductive, rules determining when to examine something, when to make a decision, can be very helpful. Putting your own personal rules in writing, into a transportable "rulebook" can be helpful. Finally, rationale needs to override emotion in all investments.

Points to Remember

As a summary, here are some of the more commonly used plays in the active part of an active investor's portfolio:

- *Play the trading range.* Active investors get to know companies and the behavior of stock prices, mainly through charting. If shares trade in a visible trading range around an appropriate valuation, active investors look to buy when the stock approaches the bottom of the range and sell near the top. Limit orders may be used to enter and exit trades, and the investor looks for signs of change in that range. Selling covered calls (Chapter 14) can also be used to turn these fluctuations into income.
- *Overbought, oversold.* Active investors look for swing trades when prices diverge substantially from fundamental value. Market events, news events, and analyst coverage often external to the company's fundamentals create these opportunities. The active investor enters these trades knowing that fundamental value provides downside risk protection, but due diligence must continually ascertain fundamental value.
- *Play the earnings announcements.* Anticipation of earnings often leads to a run-up in stock price and a subsequent, if very temporary, decline. Careful play of these fluctuations can turn into income on the "front side," often through covered call options, and buying during the sell-off. Selling short is a riskier play but is often used (the risk is that earnings are better than expected and contain no flaws).
- *Play stocks in strong or weak sectors.* Sharp-eyed investors figure out what sectors are strong (or weak) and play individual stocks in those sectors for short-term gain. Favored sectors

provide "tailwinds" for their component stocks; sectors out of favor create headwinds, though sometimes the winner in a losing sector can be amply rewarded (think Dell Computer). The premise: Strength in the sector should produce gains and reduce risk. "Even turkeys fly in a high enough wind" is part of this investing mantra.

Part V:

Blending Investments and Investing Styles

Chapter 13

Fund Investing for Active Investors

Active investing is a blended, diversified approach to investing. Like most investing approaches, active investing suggests building a diverse basket of investments. But it also goes a step further to suggest a diversification, or *blend,* of investing *styles.* Repeating a core theme: Active investing is a secondary activity in one's personal life, and the "work-life-investing" balance often requires delegating at least some tasks to professionals. Consistent with this idea, most active investors employ a mix of self-chosen and managed investments. In a sense, this diversifies the management of your investments, capturing the best of your investing ideas and the benefits brought by professional management.

Further, the active investing approach as defined here suggests stratifying your investments into a core long-term oriented *foundational* portfolio, a *rotational* portfolio tied to changes in the business cycle, and an *opportunistic* portfolio designed to turn short-term opportunities into income. For many active investors, funds or managed investments are building blocks for the foundational portfolio, while certain types of funds, mainly exchange-traded funds (ETFs) are building blocks for the rotational portfolio. In many cases, where 401(k) and similar retirement plans make up most of the foundational portfolio, funds are the only choice, as individual stocks or other investments are not offered. Bottom line: Managed fund investments are important components of most active portfolios. This chapter gives a strategic overview of managed fund investments, an explanation of tools and their use, and some ideas and wisdom about active investing with funds.

Types of Funds

"Funds," as the term is used here, include baskets of individual securities set up for an investor to buy as one security. Funds may be *actively* managed by a professional investment manager, or they may be *passively* managed—that is, individual investments are chosen according to a predefined mix (for example, the stocks in the S&P 500 index). Active managers usually are individuals with a supporting staff, analyzing individual companies with sophisticated investing tools and selecting them based on potential performance and consistency with the style of the fund being managed. Actively managed funds would normally be chosen to diversify the *management* of your investments. A passively managed fund diversifies *holdings* while moving your wealth in lockstep with the market as a whole or a key sector of the market. Both types of managed funds allow you to focus on opportunistic investments and other things besides investing.

Professionally managed funds include *mutual funds, unit investment trusts* (UITs) and *exchange-traded funds* (ETFs). There are important management style—and legal—differences between each of these types. Mutual funds make up about 90 percent of all assets invested in funds, but UITs and especially ETFs are gaining ground rapidly. Mutual funds got so large essentially by turning investments into a consumer product, complete with sales and marketing campaigns that one might associate with a typical consumer product. The dominant, open-ended funds brought investing to the masses, and the masses responded with several trillion dollars of investments in more than 9,000 different funds. But in recent years, mutual fund management scandals and an underlying mistrust of overcompensated managers have undermined public perception. As consumers become more savvy to the costs of that overhead and marketing, the tide is starting to shift. Particularly for active investors, it is shifting to other alternatives, and especially to ETFs as they become more available and better understood.

This isn't to say that all mutual funds are bad. They do offer focused professional management for investors who really want to delegate to someone else, and they also offer variety and diversification not available when picking individual companies. But active investors should understand the intricacies of mutual funds, including their costs, benefits, and role, in order to make sure that they don't invest blindly.

Mutual Funds

The mutual fund concept first hit the streets with the Investment Company Act of 1940, where pools of assets could be bundled for sale to individual investors with flow-through returns—that is, returns not taxed at the corporate level and again at the individual investor level. (One main idea was to avoid *triple* taxation—taxation at the corporate level for the individual security, taxation again at the investment company level, and yet again when distributed to the individual investor!). There were certain rules, among them were (1) at least 90 percent of investment company returns would be distributed to individuals, (2) the fund must own at least eleven different investments and 50 percent of the fund must have no single investment greater than 5 percent (achieving diversification), and (3) no single investment would comprise more than 25 percent of a portfolio (again, diversification).

Mutual funds evolved as *open-end* and *closed-end* funds. Open-end funds are capitalized just as investors invest in them: Any investor buying shares gets new shares, and when investors redeem shares the amount comes directly out of the asset base. The value of an open-end mutual fund share precisely matches the value of the underlying assets; that is to say, if you own a share of a fund with 100,000 shares, you own 1/100,000th of the fund's "basket" of investments. The *net asset value*, or NAV, is the total value of the basket measured at the end of each investing day; the per-share NAV is the price of each share and is quoted in the "mutual fund" section of the daily paper.

Closed-end funds, on the other hand, have a fixed and defined number of shares traded on an exchange much as any other share. They trade on NYSE, NASDAQ, and other exchanges. These shares are bought on a supply/demand basis, and only approximate the value of the underlying investment on a daily basis. The difference between share price and underlying investment value is known as a *premium* or a *discount*, depending on its direction. Many closed-end funds sell at a discount to NAV, making them somewhat attractive, sort of like buying a basket of securities "on sale" and giving the investor some margin of safety. Major financial newspapers list closed-end funds separately each Monday with a summary of premiums and discounts. Closed-end funds have been something of an investing backwater, though they are used to achieve international diversification (through the so-called "country funds"). The detachment of share price from underlying investment value is a little unnerving for some investors wishing to trust both fund management and the markets on which it trades. ETFs, which tie share price more directly to NAV, have become more popular.

Open-Ended Funds

Most open-ended funds are managed by such household financial brands as Fidelity, T. Rowe Price, Vanguard, and American Century—pick up any newspaper or magazine and you'll see a dozen advertisements. These big companies—some are stock-exchange-traded companies themselves—provide the research, manage the investments, and market their "services" (shares) to the public. They make money by charging management and marketing fees to investors, and their major costs are (1) internal management and research, (2) research bought from others, and (3) commissions paid to brokers and financial planners to sell their product. Families bring an assortment of funds to the market covering all styles, many sectors, and different kinds of securities, including bonds and other fixed-income investments. Most fund families allow investors to switch—or reallocate—assets between funds in the family at no cost.

Classifying Open-Ended Funds

At the highest level, funds break down into four groups, to an extent defining a fund's *profile*. *Common stock* funds invest most assets in common stocks, with some cash set aside to manage redemptions. Different common stock funds have different strategies, or *styles*. *Bond funds* carry different profiles depending on whether they invest in high-risk ("junk") or investment-grade bonds, taxable or tax-free bonds, or long- versus short-term bonds. Regardless, bond safety and fixed income are the primary objectives, although the specialized convertible bond fund provides some exposure to equity appreciation (convertible bonds can be converted to a specified number of common shares, mixing fixed income with appreciation potential). *Money market funds* invest in short-term fixed-income securities and are mainly a way to park cash with virtually no risk but also a very low return, less than 1 percent in 2004. *Balanced funds* blend one or more of the above.

Fund Styles

Style refers to the stated investment objective of a common stock fund. Traditional common stock fund styles include aggressive growth, small company growth, growth and income, international and foreign, specialty, and sector. Each of these is fairly self-explanatory. In recent years, the emergence of Morningstar as the premier mutual fund rating and information agency has given rise to a "grid" approach for classifying funds, brought forth as the "Morningstar Style Box."

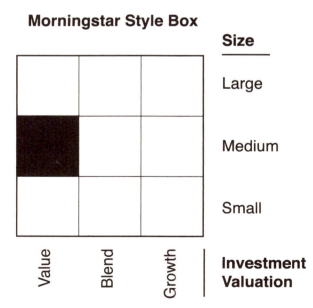

The "Y-axis" scales the fund according to the predominant size of companies invested in. Large cap funds invest primarily in companies with a market capitalization greater than $5 billion, mid cap between $1 billion and $5 billion, and small cap less than $1 billion. The "X-axis" scales the funds according to the primary criteria that must be met for investments. There are ten criteria in all, mainly financial, including P/E, price to cash flow, price to book value, growth rates, and risk. The x-axis dimensions between "value," "growth," and the in-between blend of the two. As "value" and "growth" appear as different sectors, it is obvious that Morningstar considers current financial value—not future growth potential—in its evaluation, so their definition of value differs slightly from that offered in Chapter 8, which includes growth as part of the intrinsic value.

This nine-style classification helps, but it may not be enough. Enlightened investors should look for specific statements in a fund summary or profile, as shown on Morningstar or through the Yahoo!Finance mutual fund portal. Some funds furnish specific information as to how they screen stocks; such transparency should be viewed favorably.

Fund Performance

Once a fund profile is reviewed, fund performance is the next important set of criteria. One must use caution in extrapolating historical performance into the future; in fact, studies have shown that the past is a poor indicator of the future. Why? Fund managers finding success in one set of stocks stretch too far trying to duplicate such performance in another set of stocks, or, worse yet, ride their winners too far. Be careful of advertisements suggesting high future returns based on healthy 20+ percent performance in recent years. Performance should be taken in the long term and in the context of other similar funds and the major stock indices—*comparative* performance is most important. Gains should also be taken in context of risk. There are risk measures to consider—more on that shortly—but viewing performance against funds with similar styles is another way to take risk into account. Look for sustained performance and strong performance relative to peers.

Tax Performance

For all parts of your portfolio outside of retirement assets, you should be concerned about the tax performance of a fund. Under the rules of investment companies, gains on shares sold by the fund through the year are passed through to individual owners as capital gains. Those capital gains can provide nasty year-end surprises to unsuspecting investors, particularly if the market closed the year on a weak note. Investors may pay capital gains taxes, only to have their year-end NAV end up lower than where they started (translation: diminished wealth *plus* a tax bill!). Funds that buy and sell a lot through the year have this exposure, while funds that tend to hold their investments have fewer tax consequences. Funds will disclose their annual earnings turnover; if it is 20 percent or more, that's a lot of activity and a lot of tax exposure. Again, if the fund is held in a retirement account this is a non-issue.

Fund Costs

Fund costs have become a 600-pound gorilla causing many defections from the mutual fund camp. Why? Because in this day and age of more modest returns and greater management scrutiny, investors are waking up to examine just what they are paying and

Fund Investing for Active Investors

what they get for it. When today's more modest market returns of 5–7 percent (and often less) are dampened by 5 percent sales charges, and 1–2 percent management and marketing fees, that leaves little "real" return for many investors. Driven in part by poor performance and in part by outright management scandal, the backlash against high fees has become strong.

What are these costs? At the end of the day, fund management companies must make money. They must account for their costs to manage and operate the fund, and for costs to market and sell their product to investors—a product that doesn't sell can't work. What galls a lot of investors is (1) the size and (2) the nature of some of these fees.

Sales Charges

The sales charge, known euphemistically in the industry as a *load*, is essentially a commission *you pay to the fund* for the privilege of buying in (or in some cases, cashing out). While capped by law at 8.5 percent, loads are seldom that high, but often run 4 or 5 percent. This reduction in asset value right off the bat can really dampen returns, particularly if the time value of money is considered. The good news is that investors paying an up-front load may see reduced or eliminated fees paid during their ownership, so it may work out in the long run—but only if you're committed to the fund. Some funds are offered with a back-end sales charge collected on redemption. Some of these waive this charge if the fund is held long enough—but keep in mind that if the fund performs well, the management company will collect more money (such a win-win isn't totally a bad thing). Again, you're committed to stay with the fund or lose a lot of commission dollars.

Many fund families offer several "classes" of shares—A, B, C, and sometimes even "D"—that blend various combinations of up-front sales charges, redemption charges, and combinations of these charges with ongoing, though usually reduced, management fees. And many, many more funds are "no-load," meaning such commissions aren't charged but are absorbed by fees assessed throughout your ownership.

Management Fees

Fund management companies charge a percentage for general management and research. These percentages are usually 1 percent or higher, and they are taken directly out of the NAV of the fund (not billed to investors). Such a percentage can seem small, but for a $50 billion fund like Fidelity Magellan, 1 percent could add up to $500 million annually! Even for smaller funds these percentages can add up. More actively managed funds tend to charge higher fees, but studies have shown little correlation between more active management and better performance (especially when taxes are factored in). Recently, reports of fund companies paying big brokerage houses for "research"—and getting client referrals in return—have rattled fund investors and caused them to wonder just how this management and "research" money is being spent. Reports of managers allowing special interests to trade funds "after hours" and before the daily NAV price reset, skimming perhaps a few tenths of a percent more off of the fund's NAV, have further alarmed the investing public.

12-b-1 Fees

"12-b-1," or marketing, fees have drawn the most intense spotlight in recent years. Like management fees, these fees are assessed against the fund's NAV to cover marketing expenses—mainly commissions paid to brokers and advisors bringing in new investors. Yes, existing investors are directly footing the bill to bring new investors in. 12-b-1 fees can range up to 1 percent, again a large amount of money in a big fund.

Fund Investing for Active Investors 203

Are You Getting What You Pay For?

Underperformance is one of today's chief criticisms of traditional stock mutual funds. Studies show that 70 percent of funds underperform the S&P 500 average! In other words, professional managers produce performance worse on average—and more expensive—than "buying the market." Why does this happen? First, there are the fees and costs. The 1–2 percent taken off the top adds up, as we've seen. Also, fund managers are sometimes bound by fund rules about what they can invest in. Worse, fund managers must report to their superiors, and organizational dynamics can motivate these managers to avoid doing what they can't explain to those superiors. Translation: They tend to follow what everyone else is doing. As a result, funds tend to do the same thing at the same time and to own the same stocks, and unless you're lucky enough to hold one of the first funds in, you will likely achieve subpar returns. The point: look for funds that beat the S&P 500 consistently, both in up and down markets.

The Fee "Big Picture"

Taken together, these fees can add up, especially for actively managed funds. While total fees for an index fund might be less than 0.5 percent, management and 12-b-1 fees average about 1.4 percent and can add up to almost 3 percent each year. Thus a fund that manages a 7 percent growth in NAV will take 2–3 percent and leave you with the remaining 4–5 percent. That doesn't sound bad on the surface, until you (1) look at the compound effects of this reduction (see Chapter 2), and (2) you consider that fund management companies collect these fees regardless of performance; that is, they get guaranteed payment while you take all of the risk. All of these reasons add up to considerable scrutiny. Funds with good management teams and track records may be worth the cost, but like anything else, as an investor you must evaluate value gained for value spent—in this case, on fund fees.

Risk and Risk Measures

Any investor understands the traditional risk-reward tradeoff; that is, all else being equal, larger returns require taking larger risks. For portfolio managers, managing risk involves selecting a set of investments in such a way as to get the most potential return for the least portfolio risk; that is, if an individual investment doesn't pan out, the effect on the portfolio is mitigated by performance in the other investments. The science behind risk management is complex. What's important is to understand the risk profile chosen by a mutual fund, and how that risk compares to the returns achieved. Obviously, for an individual fund, a strong return track record with modest risk is preferred to a low or erratic return profile with high risk.

Quantifying risk is extremely difficult. If you invest in a business, what is the risk, or probability, of losing on that investment, and how much will you lose? It's like forecasting the weather six months out—you just don't know. The approach used by the investing world is to measure return volatility—that is, how much returns deviate from the expected outcome. A high-risk investment has a wide range of potential outcomes, high and low. A low-risk investment has a relatively narrow range of outcomes. So the investing world looks at the *standard deviation* of the *past* performance of the investment as a proxy for future risk.

From basic statistics, standard deviation quantifies the average amount of volatility around an average. Statistically, about two-thirds of all possible outcomes occur within one standard deviation range of the average; 95 percent occur within two standard

Fund Investing for Active Investors 205

deviations, and 99 percent occur within three standard deviations. So if a fund reports a standard deviation of 5 around a value of $28, there is only a 5 percent statistical chance that the price will go below $18 or above $38. (95 percent of outcomes are projected to be between a two-standard-deviation range, or +/– $10.)

You can see the problems with standard deviation: (1) future outcomes are strictly a function of the past (the driving-with-the-rearview-mirror issue), and (2) it doesn't account for fundamental business changes or events. Yet it's a good guideline and a place to start.

Now, the next trick is to take standard deviation in context of a mutual fund. From the top of this section, a high standard deviation, or high risk, is good only if the fund is achieving high returns—otherwise, there is too much risk for the amount of return achieved and your money would be better deployed elsewhere. Mutual fund investors use the Sharpe's Ratio to relate return and risk. The formula for Sharpe's Ratio is:

Sharpe's Ratio =
(Actual Return – Risk-Free Rate of Return) / Standard Deviation

Actual return is the fund's actual performance; the "risk-free" return is a market rate without risk, usually a U.S. Treasury bond return rate. So, using Sharpe's Ratio, you can see if fund returns have (1) beaten the risk-free rate and (2) are risk-effective. A negative Sharpe's ratio indicates below risk-free returns. That's the first test. The second test is to see how the Sharpe's Ratio compares to other funds—higher ratios are better, reflecting higher returns, lower risk, or both. The higher the ratio, the better.

Fund Holdings

What does a fund actually hold in its portfolio? That's a fairly obvious test of fund suitability for most practical investors, but it's surprisingly elusive. Does the fund hold stocks that you yourself would want to hold? That's a good thing for most investors. However, there is a contrarian viewpoint to this; perhaps you want a fund that holds stocks you don't know about, or further, wouldn't buy yourself. This view follows the ideas of diversification and the delegation of some of the investing task to others—if you don't have the stomach to buy a particular stock, maybe it's okay to have an interest through your foundational fund investments, managed by someone else.

More Eggs in the Basket

Another important revelation in a fund's Top Holdings list: what percentage of the fund is made up by the top holdings? The more stocks (or bonds) held by a fund, the more diversified—but also the more that returns will look like the market average. You may be as well off with an index-based ETF. Knowledge-based fundamental investing selects the few really good companies and concentrates on them. Look for Top 10 holdings to be more than 25 percent of the fund; in fact, figures closer to 50 percent are better—a sign that management really knows what they're doing.

The problems with looking at individual holdings are transparency and timeliness. Funds normally disclose their holdings in statements once per quarter, sometimes once every six months. So by the time you find out, they may well have moved on. Secondly, most portals give only the top 10 holdings. This is useful, but doesn't tell the whole picture. That said, it's good to check holdings to evaluate congruence to your own investing tastes and to see if you're getting what you pay for from management. If their top 10 holdings are nothing but overplayed favorites like Microsoft, GE, Coca-Cola, and Exxon-Mobil, you might not be getting much for your fees and might be better off in a less expensive ETF.

Fund Management

Good management makes a difference in fund performance; active investors should take the time to find good fund managers. But it's hard to know who is, and who isn't, a good manager. Track record, or performance, is important, and reputation can also figure in. Look where the manager has been, and how long he/she has been with a particular fund. Look for evidence of authority and recognition outside the daily business of the fund. Profile statements and holdings lists can give an idea of whether the manager comes up with well-researched, creative picks or just follows the crowd. This one is tough, and the lack of fund transparency makes it tougher, but the more you can find out, the better.

Information Sources

Where do investors get all this information? Getting it isn't easy, but the Yahoo!Finance Mutual Fund portal does a good job with most fund criteria. Yahoo!Finance information is supplied by Morningstar (discussed in Chapter 4) as the leading source of mutual fund information and evaluation. Keep in mind that most information is best used *comparatively*; that is, when comparing fund choices.

The four Yahoo!Finance pages for each fund are Profile, Performance, Holdings, and Risk. Here are some things you should look for on each of them:

- *On the Profile page*—Look for style box, fund summary, portfolio turnover, fees, and expenses.
- *On the Performance page*—Look for returns, number of years up versus down, returns vs. similar funds, and key market indices.
- *On the Holdings page*—Look for Top 10 holdings, percent of fund assets, and average valuation ratios for holdings.
- *On the Risk page*—Look for standard deviation, Sharpe's Ratio.

Selecting Funds

Active investors make two decisions: (1) whether or not to invest in mutual funds and (2) if the fund path is chosen, which mutual funds to invest in. In many cases, as with 401(k) plans and "529" college savings plans, the first choice may be largely made. For more discretionary assets, think of it as a need to have professional fund managers working alongside you. Funds have several advantages including:

- *Diversification.* Multiple investments are available as a package deal.
- *Professional management.* Funds employ trained professionals with professional research tools and information; by buying a fund, you tap into these resources. Also, their perspective and methodology is at least somewhat different from your own, which may be prudent.

Fund Investing for Active Investors

- *Flexibility.* Most fund families allow easy switching between funds within a family, allowing rotation of your investments.
- *Convenience.* Funds are administratively convenient with good statements, telephone support, and automated monthly investing. Once a fund is set up, it can be left alone, allowing you to focus on other parts of your investing portfolio.

However, as an active investor you should be aware of the potential pitfalls of funds. No single fund (or single investment) will be perfect, but as an active investor you should be able to weigh the disadvantages:

- *Fees and costs.* Fees and costs can eat up returns quickly, and they may not give you your money's worth.
- *Tax consequences.* There may be significant tax exposure for funds held outside of retirement accounts or college trusts, depending on management style and "churn."
- *Overdiversification.* Some funds are just too big, and by necessity, overdiversified. You gain no advantage over buying a straight index-oriented ETF. In particular, it makes no sense to own two large cap stock funds—they probably own many of the same investments.
- *Conflicts of interest.* Like some corporate executives, not all fund managers are working on your behalf. You must develop a trust for your fund company and its individual fund managers.
- *Lack of transparency.* Related to the last point—funds are not always as forthcoming about their doings as they should be. In part, this is due to fairly lenient reporting requirements as well as a reluctance to give too much information to the competition.

At the end of the day, selecting a fund (or fund family) becomes somewhat like selecting an individual company investment. Is it a good business, and does it put its shareholder interests first? Each candidate should be investigated individually—and compared to other choices—for performance, fees and costs, holdings, churn and taxes, and more subtle factors of management competence and transparency.

Unit Investment Trusts

Unit investment trusts are legally defined investment companies with rules somewhat different from mutual funds. UITs are normally set up with a specific investing objective for a specific time frame. They usually acquire a basket of assets and hold it until the predefined liquidation date, although some have charters that allow switching or rebalancing investments under certain criteria.

Real Estate Investment Trusts, or REITs, are the most known and popular form of UITs. Real estate trusts buy a portfolio of properties, usually specific types of properties such as shopping centers, residential, commercial, or even specialized buildings such as health care facilities. They distribute income and gains to investors much as mutual funds do. REITs are measured by examining Funds From Operations (FFO), a proxy for cash flow. Some REITs are leveraged; that is, they borrow money to finance purchases, so they are exposed to lending rates, and a few are actually in the mortgage business. There are more than 200 REITs listed on the major exchanges, and a trade group portal operated by the National Association of Real Estate Trusts (NAREIT, at *www.nareit.com*) is a source for more information. As REITs trade on all major exchanges, their stocks can be examined through Yahoo!Finance and other investing services.

Fund Investing for Active Investors

REITs, and other UITs specializing in other assets such as oil, are a good addition to a foundation or rotational portfolio. They provide a way to invest in such hard assets without actually owning buildings or oil wells. They are liquid and professionally managed, taking the specialized task out of your hands.

Exchange Traded Funds

Finally, we arrive at the increasingly important subject of Exchange Traded Funds, or ETFs. They are a form of unit investment trust set up to invest in a predefined type of securities. Usually these are stocks but also can include bonds and other types of investments. Like mutual funds, ETFs allow investors to buy a basket of securities through a single investment. Through ETFs, investors can acquire "market" portfolios easily and cheaply—like the S&P 500 or a balanced NASDAQ portfolio, or they can branch out into international, specific country, or specific sector portfolios. ETFs are an increasingly important investing tool and should be considered by all active investors for foundational, rotational, and even occasionally, opportunistic portions of the portfolio.

At the time of this writing, there are 126 "listed" ETFs trading on major exchanges, primarily the "AMEX" or old American Stock Exchange, now part of NASDAQ. The investment trusts are created, managed and branded by a handful of large investment banks including Barclay's (iShares), State Street Bank (SPDRs), and Vanguard (VIPERs). Shares trade just as any other stock, and can be bought and sold throughout the day at a price closely approximating underlying NAV.

ETF Advantages

ETFs allow active investors to buy into and rotate among large sectors of the market easily and inexpensively. Since ETFs are unit trusts, there is little to no change of individual stocks owned (unless they fall out of the underlying index, merge, etc). Thus, management fees are microscopic, as low as 0.12 percent for the SPDR S&P 500 Index ETF, up to a minimal 0.50 percent for the most specialized of funds. There are no entry or exit costs save the discount broker commission. With stable portfolios there are few tax consequences; most capital gains tax is paid simply when you exit the position. Management vagaries sometimes found in traditional funds are largely nonexistent.

ETFs offer many traditional mutual fund advantages while avoiding many disadvantages. Traditional mutual funds can provide an active management team supported by professional research, but most of the other advantages—convenience, diversification—are found in ETFs too. Such characteristics play well into the needs and style of the active investor.

The ETF Store

The best way to explain the ETF universe is to show the list of funds available. Note how they break down into index funds, international, and several series of sector funds. Sector funds can either cover higher-level "style box" sectors such as Large Cap Value or Large Cap Growth, or can "drill down" into industry sectors such as biotechnology, energy or pharmaceuticals. International ETFs can be region or country specific or provide broader international exposure. The same details that can be captured for mutual funds can also be found for ETFs—including profile, performance, holdings, and risk—on Yahoo!Finance by simply entering the ticker symbol.

Chapter 14

Investing Potpourri: Specialized Tools for Both Sides of the Market

Not all stocks go up. Not all markets go up. That obvious truth presents a challenge for the active investor—the all-important question of *how to play defense.* How do you achieve better-than-market returns in a down market or a no-growth, sideways market? Part of the answer is to ride the strongest horses—to pick investments in the best businesses that prosper even in the worst of times—but, in practice, this is a difficult promise to keep, and bad markets will sour even the sweetest stocks. The answer also doesn't lie in putting money in a bank or money market fund earning 2 percent or less—nearly equivalent to stuffing it under your mattress to be eaten away by inflation.

Active investors must find more active ways to play defense or even profit from weak markets. To put it in more strategic terms, active investors must learn to *hedge* against market failures and failures in individual stocks. The term *hedging* refers to entering contrary positions that profit as other investments lose, sort of like an insurance policy against market "casualties." Beyond hedging, there are ways to turn future growth potential into current income—sort of a bird-in-hand proposition boosting returns and augmenting individual income obtained elsewhere. This chapter examines the active investor's use of some of these tools, including equity options, index options, bonds, commodities, and international stocks.

Before we proceed, it should be noted that some of these tools and techniques are more complex and sophisticated than most employed by individual investors. However, when clearly understood and used correctly, these tools can actually serve to reduce overall portfolio risk. Active investors should be well prepared and should practice using these tools, especially options, before deploying them widely in their portfolios.

Equity Options

Equity options are derivative securities—that is, securities whose value is tied to an underlying stock. This may be a scary term, as most have heard about the fast-paced, risky world of derivatives used in high-flying financial circles. Derivatives are no more than a way for investors to pass risk back and forth to each other, sort of like an insurance market within the securities market. Depending on how derivative "cards" are played, you can pass some risk to someone else, paying a modest premium for the privilege. But equity investing has both upside and downside potential, unlike the real world of event risk insurance covered by insurance, which only guards against downside "casualties." You may choose to transfer some of your potential upside gain to someone else—this time *collecting* the premium. Essentially, you are selling, not buying, the insurance—isn't it nice for once to be on the receiving end of such a transaction? Equity options essentially allow you to play the insurance game—in many ways—to strategic advantage.

Equity options were once reserved primarily for large institutional traders and available only for stocks traded on the largest companies. But in the past twenty years, markets for "listed," or exchange-traded, options have flourished. Options can be bought and sold for thousands of companies, large and small. The Chicago Board Options Exchange (CBOE) is the largest trading venue, but smaller exchanges, like the Pacific and Philadelphia Stock Exchanges, also trade many series, or "chains" of options.

Types of Equity Options

Equity options come in two basic types: *puts* and *calls*. A call option is a contract to *buy* 100 shares of an underlying stock at a specific price on or before a specific date. The price is known as the *strike price*, the date is known as the *expiration*. So if you buy one *XYZ June 30 call*, you are buying a contract that allows you to buy 100 shares of XYZ at $30 each anytime before the June expiration. What do you pay for that call option contract? Similar to insurance, you pay an amount known as a *premium*, determined by several factors expanded upon below. And when do they expire in June? Equity options expire on the Saturday following the third Friday of each month, meaning that the price at the end of trading that Friday determines the final value of the option. A put option turns the tables the other way: An *XYZ June 30 put* contract gives you the right to sell 100 shares of XYZ at $30 on or before the expiration date.

What Are Equity Options Worth?

In the above *XYZ June 30 call* example, it is easy to see that the option has value at expiration if the stock closes above $30, and it is worthless if the option closes below that level. Likewise, the *XYZ June 30 put* has value if the stock closes *below* $30. But what is that option worth in May? In April? That's where much of the interest in options arises.

The value of an option is determined by three factors: (1) the difference between the current stock price and the strike price, (2) the *time to expiration*, and (3) the *volatility* of the underlying investment. Obviously, if the current price of a security is above the strike price, the call option will have value and more value the larger the difference, while the put option has no theoretical value. But this value, sometimes known as *intrinsic* value, is just one factor. The longer the time to expiration, the more events can occur that may change the fortunes of the underlying investment, and the more chance the stock price has to exceed the strike price. Thus, an option expiring nine months from now is better than one expiring next week, and it will be priced accordingly. Finally, the volatility, or variability, of the underlying stock influences the value of the option. A stock that regularly moves between 20 and 40 has more potential to produce winners for strike-price-30 call buyers than one that only moves between 28 and 32. That stronger possibility to gain 10 points—40 less 30—will drive premiums higher for more volatile stocks.

These factors play together in mathematically complex ways to drive the price of options. Options "in the money" or "at the money" will be worth more than options deeply "out of the money." In the above XYZ scenario, a June 45 call option has little intrinsic value at the end of May. But if it's only January, there is a stronger possibility that favorable events could drive the price higher, and if there is track record of volatility or unpredictability, that call contract will have still more value. Because of leverage— the ability to turn small investments into large gains—out-of-the-money options will get a stronger time and volatility premium. Since options are traded securities, someone has to sell the option that you buy, and that seller doesn't want to give up that above-45

Investing Potpourri

potential gain for just pennies, while likewise the buyer is getting a chance—albeit a smaller one—to achieve a huge percentage gain. For "in the money" options—say XYZ 25 calls, the time and volatility value will be relatively less. Why? Because the investor must pay more to enter the position, and is risking more since they could lose the entire larger position.

How these factors affect option prices is hard to tease out until you look at real scenarios. If a stock is selling at $29.50 in April, a June 30 call might sell for $1.50. This is all time and volatility premium—but since the underlying price is so close to the strike price, the chances of success are higher, thus the price reflects a 5 percent premium over the two months. A June 25 call might sell for $5.50. The intrinsic value is $4.50 (determined by $29.50 – $25), and the time/volatility premium is reduced to $1 because of the smaller leverage and higher risk incurred by the investor (the risk of losing $5.50, instead of $1.50, in the June 30 call example). The June 45 call might sell for $0.40. This is all time and volatility premium. Since the stock has to run 15.5 points to hit the money, paying 50 cents seems much more expensive than the $1.50 paid for the June 30 call, where the stock has to gain only 50 cents to finish in the money. This illustrates the "leverage" effect.

Time Value of Options—Illustrated

The effect of time to expiration on option values is hard to explain in words, but it is easier to comprehend with **Figure 14.1** (see page 218). The picture shows how option values increase as time-to-expiration increases, but at a decreasing rate. Why? We'll avoid technical explanations, but observe that five days is five times one day, while ten days is only twice five days, fifteen days is only 50 percent more than ten days, and so forth. Each increment in time is priced in accordingly.

Figure 14.1 Time to Expiration and Option Value

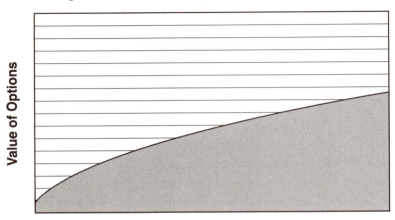

Option Chains

An *option chain* is simply the list of available options on a security. For XYZ stock, there may be put and call options trading at 15, 20, 25, 30, 35, 40, and 45. Whether an option is available depends on the interest of market makers and the market in general—there simply isn't enough interest in a June 60 call for a stock trading in a 25–30 range for market makers to set one up. But as the price approaches 60, that option may appear, and it *will* appear if it becomes the next strike—that is, if the stock closes above 55.

Some options for more popular stocks may trade in $2.50 increments, and some lower-priced, highly active stocks like Lucent Technologies may trade options in $1 increments. Finally, more active stocks will have options trading in monthly expiration increments at least for the next three months; thereafter, they trade in three-month increments. Some chains trade in June-September-December increments, some in July-October-January,

Investing Potpourri

some in August-November-February. Finally, there are longer-term options known as "LEAPs," or Long Term Equity Appreciation contracts, which have expiration increments up to three years out, usually expiring in January of that year, as in a January 2008 call. Obviously, LEAPS will have a high premium for time value. LEAPS provide a good way to buy into a company's fortunes for a long period with relatively little cash outlay, but the high time premium can make this expensive.

The Black-Scholes Model

Seasoned option investors are familiar with the standard "Black-Scholes" mathematical model considering distance to strike price, time, volatility, and leverage. The mechanics are beyond our scope here, but most option trading platforms give a Black-Scholes theoretical valuation for each option to compare with the actual market price. While useful, the behavior of prices is best understood by visual experience gained by examining the option *chain* over time.

Trading Options

Options are bought and sold on option exchanges much like stocks. Each option has a quoted bid and offer price, and market orders will get those prices. There is no "Level II" quote queue. Most options are traded with the market maker, not with other buyers and sellers. Options trade in 5-cent increments—that is, $1.50, $1.55, $1.60—and typically have large spreads between bid and ask. The minimum spread is 5 cents, of course, and spreads can range to 25 cents or even more. So option investors must be aware of these larger markups. Further, most option commissions are higher than stock commissions; many brokers use options to recover revenue lost with "loss-leader" stock trading commissions. That said, if you plan to trade a lot of options, most brokers have favorable option commissions, perhaps $10 plus $1 per contract. Otherwise, you may pay $30, $40 or even more per options trade. Like everything else, wise comparison shopping helps, and remember to look beyond the commission—information resources and telephone support are important for options trading, too. Most brokerage Web sites and the CBOE Web site *(www.cboe.com)* offer solid facts and tutorials, and options trading is one good place where phone support offered by your broker can really help.

Writing Covered Calls

Earlier material showed the nature of buying call contracts—that is, contracting to buy 100 shares of XYZ at $30 by the third Friday of June. That trade "wins" if the price closes above $30 (actually, above $30 plus the premium paid for the option and brokerage commission) by that date.

But what if you *sell* that call option? What if you *collect* a $1.50 premium for allowing someone to buy 100 shares of XYZ at $30 by June *from you*? Picture yourself as the green-visored dealer or insurance agent on the other side of the table, and you get the idea. Collecting money by selling options becomes a major play for the active investor, generating both short-term income and downside protection.

Here's how it works: Buy 100 shares of XYZ as you would normally buy any stock, that is, as a rational purchase of business assets at an attractive price. Then turn around and sell a *covered* call option (*covered* by your ownership of the underlying security), usually for a strike price slightly above your purchase price. Why slightly above? To get the most time and volatility premium, and to "lock in" a sale price, if the stock rises above your purchase price. So you make money on the premium and on a small amount of price appreciation. As an example, buy 100 XYZ at $29.50 in May and sell a June 30 call at $1.50, and collect $1.50 plus the 50-cent gain from $29.50 to $30 if the stock appreciates to $30 or higher. You don't have to *buy* the stock outright—this also works for stocks already held in your portfolio.

What are you actually doing? You are giving up the potential of a larger future gain—say, if the stock rises to $34 or $35, for a more certain $1.50 collected at the time the option is sold. You're giving up what might happen in favor of a certain current income—a proverbial bird in hand. At the same time, you still retain normal investment risk, as the stock price might decline. But even this risk is diminished. If the stock you bought drops to $28, you still break even, as you sold a call for $1.50 when you bought the shares at $29.50. And what about the return on your investment? If the stock price stays unchanged through the period, you collect $1.50 on a $29.50 investment—a return slightly exceeding 5 percent in one month. (This omits the effects of commissions, which are usually significant enough to take into account.) Finally, if the stock drops further, you lose, but again, the losses are tempered by the $1.50 premium collected.

Writing Covered Calls in Practice

Writing covered calls is a key "opportunistic" strategy to improve returns by generating short term income and to play defense by reducing losses. While most people think derivatives and options are risky and "not for them," writing covered calls effectively reduces your risk by transferring it to someone else. However, "gains forfeited" can be significant, and if you take away the upside on *all* of your investments, particularly with options written for long expirations, that can severely affect long-term performance, particularly since downside exposure is still retained.

Writing covered calls on a limited portion of your portfolio is usually best. That way you still preserve upside gains on much of the portfolio. Some stocks may be acquired just to write covered calls; this works especially well on more volatile, lower-priced stocks. The volatility creates higher premiums, and the lower price tends to reduce downside risk (although by no means eliminates it). Look for stocks that have good fundamental value (again, providing a safety net) and high option premiums (3–5 percent for one month expiration is good). You might acquire them and hope for a small gain before selling the call, but doing it immediately is a more disciplined approach preferred by many active investors. If a stock rises above the stock price, let it go. Find another stock. Don't chase it by covering, or buying back, the call—you'll lose eventually and pay the dealer markup to boot. If a stock drops below your breakeven point, try to resist the temptation to write another call at a strike below your purchase price—"locking in" loss positions is usually not a good idea, although it is sometimes warranted in very poor markets.

Don't Get Caught Naked

What if you sell a call option on a stock you don't own? There is no obligation to own the underlying stock, but there is an obligation to deliver that stock at the strike price to the option buyer. Sure, you can collect the premium without any commitment of capital (the highest possible return on investment!). This is called selling a "naked" call. What if the stock shoots skyward? You're exposed to the entire, unlimited gain. Some gutsy investors sell naked calls, particularly at earnings announcements and similar times, but this takes a day trader's guts and then some.

Investing Potpourri

Among the best uses of covered calls is to write, or sell, them when underlying stocks already in the portfolio reach the high end of recognizable trading ranges. If more than 100 shares of the underlying stock are held, selling calls on a portion—perhaps half—of the position captures some income while preserving some of the growth opportunity. Finally, look for opportunities to use covered calls to "harvest" income and hedge potential losses from special situations like earnings announcements or short-term upside moves from takeover rumors and similar. The strategy list is too long for a full treatment here; this gives an idea how this powerful tool is used, and with practice, you'll get good at it.

Writing Covered Calls, Illustrated

Figure 14.2 shows this transaction graphically:

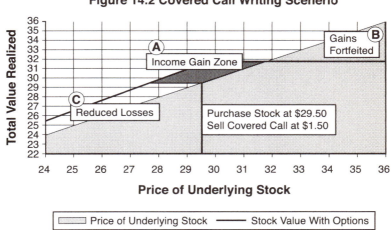

You buy 100 shares of XYZ at $29.50 and sell a June 30 call contract for $1.50. The larger triangle shows the possible price outcomes without selling the option—you may realize any value along the sloping line. By selling the option, you transfer a possibility for larger gains (B), receiving current income as compensation. The total value of this investment at different price points is represented by the heavy "stock value with option" line. If the stock price goes below $28, you'll lose, but the losses will be reduced by the option premium collected (C). At price points close to $29.50, you gain income (from the premium) beyond any loss in the underlying equity value, a scenario that occurs at any price point above $28. The parallelogram (A) represents the "sweet spot" of this transaction; that is, you pocket the income, forgo no larger gains, and incur no net depreciation of your capital. Most likely you will turn around and repeat the transaction once the third Friday of June passes, collecting another premium for the next option period. If all goes right, sustained short-term income can be generated from your investments.

Buying Puts

Puts are the right to *sell* a given number of shares at a price by an expiration date. Buying a put is most analogous to buying ordinary casualty insurance as you might do in daily life. If you buy 100 XYZ at $29.50, you might consider buying a June 25 put—the right to sell at $25 by the third week of June. That option gains intrinsic worth when XYZ drops below $25, and so far as your portfolio is concerned, gives you a downside "floor" for that stock. Put buyers are looking for peace of mind, although during tempestuous markets, when most people think about buying puts, the premiums go up because everyone wants to buy puts. So puts are most cost effective as insurance when markets are going up. The premium paid, however, is real cash, and it will diminish your returns in a steady or rising market.

Many active investors buy a few puts here and there just for some protection and peace of mind, usually far out of the money to avoid large cash outlays. Many investors buy puts covering the broader market—on stock indices—for instance. Some put buyers will take large positions far out of the money in expectation that even a small move downward will produce gains in put prices; the goal is to sell when the put moves from 10 cents to 20 cents (a 100 percent gain), not when the put reaches an in-the-money state.

Buying Calls

In a way, the call buyer takes on more risk by receiving the risk transferred by the call seller. Buy an out-of-the-money call, and unless the stock rises past the stock price, you lose everything. But you also gain leverage—buy that XYZ June 30 call for $1.50, and if the stock moves to $35 (a 17 percent gain) you realize a value of $5, a more than 300 percent gain. Buying an in-the-money call reduces the risk of losing everything, but if the stock declines, you lose *more*.

Buying calls, in one sense, is a risk-reducing play. When you buy a call, the premium is the maximum amount you risk. So if you buy the XYZ June 30 calls at $1.50, that is the maximum amount you can lose, whereas if you buy the stock outright, you can lose the entire share value, $29.50 in the example. However, as seen earlier, the probability of losing $1.50 is higher buying the option; buying the option loses $1.50 if the stock closes at 30 or below, while the stock must close at $28 to lose $1.50 buying the stock.

Many active investors buy calls when stocks get oversold or hit the bottom end of trading ranges. Some prefer to buy out-of-the-money calls to gain the leverage and, just like with puts, capture small gains even if the option remains out of the money. Some active investors buy in-the-money calls as an alternative to buying shares. Because of time value, these calls tend to decline in value more slowly than the underlying stock, providing some near-term downside protection. Finally, some investors buy LEAPS to take a position without laying out the entire share price of the stock. Keep in mind that the main risk of options comes from the time element. When buying a stock, there is no time limit to achieve a gain, as you own it forever. With an option, on the other hand, the stock must perform in the given time. So while you risk less capital, you (1) pay a risk premium and (2) incur the risk of time.

Writing Puts

Writing, or selling, puts means that you are contracting to allow someone else to sell stock *to you* at a given price. If you write an XYZ June 30 put, you promise to pay $30 for 100 shares of the put buyer's stock. They are buying insurance for you. You collect the premium but may get stuck with 100 shares if the price stays below $30. Writing puts is a good cash-generating strategy if you plan to invest in a stock anyway and have the funds available. Instead of buying the stock and laying out $29.50 (in our example) you sell the put and collect $1.50. The downside risks are (1) the price drops to $25, raising the put value to $5, a 300 percent loss on your side (since you are "short" the position and someone must pay someone else $30 for a $25 stock) and (2) you give up appreciation above $30 between now and expiration. If the stock climbs to $35, your profit is limited to $1.50, whereas you would have cleared $5.50 ($35 − $29.50) if you had bought the stock.

Writing puts works as a way to enhance return for otherwise idle cash, and as a way to play stocks oversold or at the bottom end of a trading range. One strategy is to write the put, buy the

Investing Potpourri

stock if it finishes below the strike, and turn around and write a covered call against that stock at the same strike price.

Using Options Strategically

There are many straightforward ways to use equity options to play with risk profiles and enhance returns. Writing covered calls is probably the most straightforward and easiest-to-learn path to enhancing returns. Once the techniques outlined above are under your belt, there are various *combination* strategies—ways to combine option plays—that can further enhance returns and reduce risk. Spreads involve buying one option and selling another on the same security, usually at a different strike price and sometimes using a different expiration date. *Spreads* play with the time premium to achieve profits. A "bull spread," for example, involves buying an in-the-money call with relatively less time premium and selling an out-of-the-money call with greater time premium. Such a position is considered covered, since you have a play going both ways.

Straddles are another popular technique, where you simultaneously sell a put *and* a call at the same price or around a range, thus collecting *two* premiums. The hope is that the stock ends up right where you start. If it doesn't, you have the downside protection of two premiums; that is, if the stock drops, you won't lose net money unless it drops the value of both premiums. Selling *covered* straddles reduces risk and works well. In this technique, you buy 200 shares, sell 2 calls and 2 puts. If the stock rises, the put will expire and you'll sell your 200 shares at a modest profit, collecting that profit plus the two premiums. If the stock drops, you'll buy 200 more shares, owning 400 total, but the two premiums collected offset the cost of doing so, and you can turn around and sell 4 calls on the resulting position. This is best done on stocks you consider good values and wouldn't mind owning anyway.

Such a strategy as covered straddles requires a little more experience and "pencil" work to pull off successfully; simple covered call writing is probably the best place for the new active investor to start, with buying puts as insurance not far behind. It's easy to see how you can use your opportunistic portfolio to go into the insurance business, collecting good premiums each month through the sale of options, and buying insurance where appropriate to hedge against the worst in the markets.

The concept and use of equity options strengthens with time and practice. Novice active investors should observe these instruments and their behavior over time, and begin with modest investments. Over time, you will develop your own comfort zone for issues such as whether to trade in-the-money or out-of-the-money options, whether to sell covered calls or buy puts, and what time horizons to use. Investors learn price behavior over time, and to look for "knees" in the option pricing curve—where the option price starts to decline more rapidly as expiration is approached or where it starts to change more rapidly as the strike price is approached. (See **Figure 14.1** for an example of the "knee"—where the price change steepens close to "time zero.") Note that this is conceptual and there is no place to actually view this chart in the available option trading tools, but one gets a good feel in practice. Active option investors become familiar with certain stocks and their options and many "play" short-term equity options on them each month. Others use longer-term options as stock surrogates or to hedge against major downside market activity. The cliché "to each his own" applies well to the strategic use of options.

Index and Sector Options

Index options extend the concept of equity options into market sectors and collective baskets of stocks. Thus, it becomes possible to buy or write calls on the S&P 500 as a whole, or virtually any other component of the market. As with equity options, active investors use these options to hedge against other investments and to generate short-term cash. There are options traded on major stock market indices or averages, and options are also traded on many ETFs, thus giving active investors several ways to use options on major segments of the market.

Index Options

Many financial institutions and stock exchanges themselves publish a series of indices tracking the collective behavior of a certain basket of stocks. The S&P 500 Index (SPX) is a composite of the 500 stocks designated by Standard & Poor's, Inc. to represent the market. The S&P 100 (OEX) is a smaller basket. There is a NASDAQ 100 (NDX), several Dow market indices, Russell 2000 stocks, and the Major Market Index, following large-cap stocks across the market (XMI), and so forth. More specific sectors are tracked by such indices as the Semiconductor Index (SOXX), the AMEX Pharmaceutical Index (DRG), and the Morgan Stanley Cyclical Index (CYC). There are indices covering Europe, Japan, and other sectors. Indices can be tracked on Yahoo!Finance generally by adding a "^" to the symbol (as in ^SPX, ^CYC). Yahoo!Finance lists the components of each index and its price behavior, and includes charts and options chains.

These indices aren't bought and sold as securities but are represented as calculated numbers and updated on a real-time basis through the day. However, investors can buy and sell and options on these indices; paying or collecting a premium against the future price movements of these underlying indices. Unlike equity options, which "deliver" through a purchase or sale of the underlying shares, index option are settled using cash; that is, if you write an S&P 500 call and the index rises above the strike price, an amount of cash corresponding to the value of the option at expiration is transferred out of your account. There are no underlying securities bought or sold.

Strategies for using index options vary, but one of the more popular plays is a cash-generating hedge against a broad market decline. You build a well-chosen and diversified portfolio of stocks, then "go to market" to write an S&P 500 call. The S&P 500 call contract is usually near but out of the money, usually for a short term, with an expiration two weeks to a month out. If the S&P is at 1095 and you sell an 1100 call, it might sell for $9 or $10. These options are quoted much like equity options—contracts are for 100 units. So you collect $900, or $1,000 less commission. If the market declines or stays the same through expiration, you collect the income. If the S&P 500 rises to, say, 1115, you would be liable for $1,500 (1115 – 1100 x 100). But your portfolio—at least in theory—will have gone up, offsetting your losses. So if the market stays unchanged, you collect income with no harm to your underlying investments. If it declines, you lose on the underlying investments but the loss is dampened by the cash premium collected; and if it goes up, your loss is offset by the rise in your underlying portfolio. In general, this all works well—unless the stocks in your portfolio fare worse than the market averages. As an active investor you have to keep your eye on this risk factor.

Active investors can use technology index options to hedge large commitments to technology stocks or can buy index options in, say, pharmaceuticals, for a defensive play (remembering that healthcare and many consumer stocks tend to fare well in down

Investing Potpourri

markets). Some investors buy deep out-of-the-money puts, usually for modest premiums, just in case another major event—like a terrorist attack—roils the market. Such a purchase is a pure insurance play. Like equity options, newly active investors should carefully watch the behavior of these instruments and perhaps do a few practice trades before diving in.

Equity Options on Exchange Traded Funds

Options are traded on most ETFs, and, as with index options, active investors can use them to hedge, generate cash, or gain long-term exposure to a market or market segment. As ETFs represent diversified portfolios, price movements are relatively modest compared to individual stocks, so premiums are relatively low. Still, covered call options can be used to generate some income against ETF holdings in a foundation or rotational portfolio.

What is "VIX"?

"VIX," or Volatility IndeX, originates and is traded on the American Stock Exchange. But unlike other indices, it doesn't represent an underlying market or basket of stocks; rather, it represents the average volatility of the market over a set period of time as a single number, which roughly corresponds to the percentage fluctuation. Can you buy and sell options on "VIX"? No, but it serves as a guide to overall market volatility—and thus the price of options. A VIX greater than 20 implies high volatility, thus signaling option premiums are high, and signaling a good time to write or *sell* options. A VIX below 15 is low, signaling a good time to buy options. The short-term VIX *trend* also provides good signals. Many investors consider an increasing VIX a sign of a market trend reversal. Active option investors can track VIX regularly on Yahoo!Finance ^VIX to gauge periods of option opportunity.

Many investors use longer-term call options to take a position, with relatively low cash outlay, in a sector, or to hedge against a major decline. ETF options are also a good way to play a vastly oversold market or downward "spike." If the markets take a major spill, one can buy a call option on a SPDR (S&P 500 ETF) or QQQ (NASDAQ 100, known as "cubes") ETF. If the index rebounds there is good upside potential; if it doesn't or if it declines further, you are only out the premium paid. Keep in mind that, as with all options, the greater the volatility, the higher the premium paid.

Commodities

As one travels through the list of stock alternatives, conversations, especially among sophisticated investors, usually find their way to commodities. Commodity investments "securitize" major economic inputs, including raw materials and money itself in the form of interest rates and foreign currencies. Commodity investors buy futures *contracts,* which are similar to options but control much larger amounts of the underlying asset and are usually bought on margin. Because of this leverage and the pure supply-demand nature of raw materials, futures prices can be highly volatile. Commodity prices can spike—up or down—rapidly based on rumors or on minute changes in external factors like weather and war. Over time, high commodity prices have consistently brought more supply to market—driving the price down eventually (as with gold and oil in recent years) causing many futures investors playing rapid increases to eventually lose. In short, risks—and rewards—to individual investors are quite high. At minimum, one must know what they are doing and be able to track these markets closely; it is beyond the scope of most "working" active investors.

Investing Potpourri

Still, it is compelling in today's economy to have at least some stake in the price of raw materials and business inputs. Without that stake, you are vulnerable to price spikes; the rest of your portfolio will suffer if input prices drive down profits, as happened with oil in 2004. Many investment professionals recommend having at least 10 percent of a portfolio tied to commodities to provide just such a hedge.

So how can you do this without incurring the risks and headaches of trading commodity futures? As yet, the markets haven't provided any real pure way to play commodity prices through an index, but there are a few ways you can come close:

1. *Buy stocks in commodity producers.* Gold mining shares are the purest example, but energy and other mining companies qualify. You get the play in the underlying commodity, but you are also subject to the quality of their assets and management.

2. *Buy ETFs in commodity sectors.* Energy SPDRs (XLE) and SPDR Materials (XLB) are examples. Now you have the fortunes of many companies standing between you and the base commodity, but it is an easy way to play.

3. *Buy commodity mutual funds.* There are a handful of mutual funds set up to trade commodities and commodity derivatives. As commodities require active management, fees can be high.

4. *Buy country funds or ETFs for commodity-producing countries* like Canada, Mexico, and other Latin American countries. This introduces other risks—political and currency—and they aren't pure plays, for stocks in companies outside of commodity producers are held.

A well-diversified and protected portfolio probably contains at least some exposure to raw materials and other commodities, but these are tricky investments in the best of times and may be an area for professional guidance.

> **Lower the River If You Can't Raise the Bridge**
>
> Another way to insulate your investments against the vagaries of raw materials prices is simply to avoid stocks of companies overly dependent on raw materials. You may not gain on a raw material price spike, but avoiding such energy consumers as airlines or chemical producers may be a good idea for foundation portfolios, particularly in today's supply-demand uncertainty.

Bonds

Arguably, bonds have a place in an active portfolio—the $64,000 question is *what* place and *what kinds* of bonds? The world of bond investing is tricky and frankly not transparent; bonds are still mainly the province of large institutional investors. Information sources aimed at individual investors are largely nonexistent, so "active" bond investing is almost impossible. Still, bonds do bring stability and income to a portfolio, and they are usually safer than stocks. Most financial advisors recommend exposures of 20 to 40 percent of a portfolio in bond or other fixed-income securities, with the percentage growing as one approaches retirement or other significant expense, like college. Bonds are not as vulnerable to economic downturns, and they may actually benefit if such a downturn results in lower interest rates (which drive bond prices higher) as seen in a major way in the 2000–2003 time frame. But often, just as people see the light and decide to switch to bonds, it is too late. Inflated bond prices created by low interest rates or market safety concerns are vulnerable to higher

Investing Potpourri

interest rates, especially bonds with long-term maturities, and the meager returns realized are more than offset by the downside risk.

Does this sound scary? It is. Active bond investing really requires knowing what you're doing. Most individual investors don't have large enough portfolios—let alone enough information—to trade individual bonds successfully. As a result, most active investors will look for U.S. Treasury bonds or certain types of bond funds, usually for the foundation portfolio.

A Bond Alternative—Paying Off Your House

If you're looking for a way to achieve a bond-like return and stability in your investing portfolio, consider paying off your home mortgage. A mortgage is essentially a bond someone buys from you; you pay fixed interest to that investor. If that bond disappeared, you would save that interest. Does it make sense to buy an investment bond, collect 4.5 percent interest, and then pay 6 percent on your mortgage? Possibly not. The old wisdom held that paying off a mortgage reduced liquidity—you would have trouble getting cash to meet an emergency. But with today's home equity credit lines, that risk has largely disappeared. So your home can be part of your foundation portfolio. Note: The interest saved should stay in your investment portfolio. Spending it loses the advantage.

Active investors need to look for shorter maturities to reduce vulnerability to interest rate cycles and for the tax preference provided by municipals. It is simply too hard to know enough to engage in the risk of individual high-yield, or "junk" issues, and funds specializing in these issues usually have high costs, offsetting the benefit of going the "junk" route. Closed-end municipal bond funds, sold for issues in a number of individual states like New York, California, and Illinois, provide federal/state tax-free status and, considering normal tax rates, give a relatively healthy net yield with relatively little risk.

Treasuries and TIPS

Simple Treasury bonds, with two-to-five year maturities, provide decent risk-free return with little risk of price depreciation (they will be paid back in full in two to five years). Knowing that inflation is the chief nemesis of bonds, since inflated dollars repaid later are worth less, a relatively new Treasury product known as "TIPS"—for Treasury Inflation Protection Securities—has come on strong in recent years. TIPS provide a modest return but also are paid back at an inflation-indexed value, so that a 2 percent TIP may equate to a 5 percent bond if one expects a 3 percent inflation rate. Of course, with the risk of higher inflation removed, the "real" value may be higher. TIPS should be investigated as a cornerstone of the foundation portfolio, with maturities geared to major financial demands like retirement. They provide a much-needed protection against inflation as almost no other investment does. More on U.S. Treasury securities can be found at *www.ustreas.gov*.

International Investments

Individual investors are constantly coached on the virtues of diversifying internationally; that is, not putting all their eggs in the U.S. basket. True, such diversification is theoretically a good idea—as seen by some episodes during the past fifteen years where international prosperity was accompanied by a faltering United States. However, the barriers to savvy international investing are

Investing Potpourri

severe, for it is difficult to develop expertise on overseas companies and markets from where most of us sit. International companies often have complex organizations, many with rules and laws different from ours. Accounting and reporting standards are different. Throw in currency risk and cultural barriers, and the game gets vary hard. Many investors simply stick to picking good companies in the U.S. and leave the international sector to others. Guru Warren Buffett made news by making his first foreign investment in PetroChina, and with the supply-demand situation with China and oil this wasn't hard to see. So how do you get international diversification, if you decide you need it at all?

Closed-end country funds and region/country ETFs are one straightforward way to participate in international economies. A foundation investment in a few generalized funds makes sense; picking specific countries may increase returns, but it also involves some political risk in those countries.

One very logical way to build international exposure into an active portfolio is to invest in U.S. companies that do a lot of overseas business. Those companies have the know-how to do business overseas and hedge currency fluctuations. They'll help insulate your portfolio against U.S. downturns by capitalizing on exports to stronger foreign economies. In addition, they protect your portfolio, as a weak U.S. economy usually results in lower interest rates, which results in a lower dollar, which turns into stronger dollar-denominated overseas sales. Companies like IBM, Hewlett-Packard, Caterpillar, and many other industrial capital-goods producers have significant international businesses, often more than half of sales. As such, they provide quality international diversification without some of the risks inherent in selecting foreign companies.

Chapter 15

Putting Active Investing into Practice: Principles and Examples

Now that the "tour" through the main principles and techniques of active investing is complete, it's time to rewind, review, and offer some practical advice on becoming an active investor, or improving your practice if you are already active.

Rewinding the Video: Reviewing Active Investing

Active investing has been defined as a blended investing strategy invoking an assortment of existing investing techniques across a segmented portfolio to modestly exceed average market returns. Although certain parts of the portfolio may be delegated to others, you are in charge. And to the extent other commitments allow, you direct a major portion of the investing decisions. Active investing is as much a *thought process* as a specific set of investing strategies and tactics.

The Goal: Enhanced Returns, Reduced Risk

The stated purpose of active investing is not to double your money or produce a six-figure income by trading stocks for two hours each morning. Rather, active investors strive to reduce risk and enhance returns. How? By using value principles to provide safety nets and enhance long-term return prospects. By capturing short-term income opportunities offered by market distortions and risk transfer mechanisms like equity and index options. By staying agile, keeping tabs on economic, market, and business conditions, and deploying your capital appropriately. The phrase "active investing" may seem more appropriate to the hare than the tortoise in the proverbial race. But in reality, the active investor is a well-guided tortoise, one that stays the course without wandering off into the woods, one that grabs "low-hanging fruit" from the trailside while not straying from fundamental goals or principles. Active investors work hard to avoid losses and harvest gains, and they are satisfied with hitting singles and doubles here and there to achieve returns just a few percentage points ahead of the market and the economy as a whole.

Blended Strategy

Active investing blends investment types and investment platforms to optimize results. Active investors use different types of stocks—growth, income, value—from different business sectors—consumer goods, capital goods, technology—and different types of investments—stocks, mutual funds, exchange-traded funds, bonds, commodities and commodity derivatives, options—and a mix of self-directed and professional management to achieve their goals. Active investing is not a singular style or investing approach, and it is most certainly not a panacea, a "sure thing" whiz-bang get-rich-quick solution to all of your financial problems.

Enlightened Investing

Any business decision—even choosing your next house painter—is fundamentally rooted in rationale. Rationale is fundamental to active investing. Investments are viewed as commitments of capital into an understood medium, where the upside and downside risks and risk-reward profile are appraised, where reasonable goals are set and monetized when met. Active investors are tuned in to the economy, the markets, and their businesses at a multidimensional level—not just to the stock price and its movements, but also to the financials, marketplace performance, and management of the business and the industry in which companies do business. Economic signals are tracked closely for signs of change and impact on specific industries. The active investor stays on top not only of current status but also of *change* and *change prospects* in each business, industry, and set of investments as a whole. This "enlightenment" is achieved using an assortment of daily and weekly "reads" of online and print media, and it is carried out with discipline and efficiency one would expect from our proverbial tortoise.

Value Orientation

Touched on already, the active investor is fundamentally a value investor, judging investments as a commitment of capital to a business they would just as soon own themselves. Judged this way, investors are most concerned about every aspect of future performance and cash rewards for that performance. They would never buy into a company with weak returns, an insatiable appetite for still *more* capital, or a poor or deteriorating market position or customer base. That said, active investors look not only for fundamental value, but as any bargain hunter in any marketplace, they look for a reasonable *price*. Situations where the price of a company, sometimes tainted by near term distortions, underestimates future prospects, are preferred, and taking these positions serves to minimize downside risk. And value is not just a current phenomenon; more often than not it is defined by the growth prospects—the prospects for appreciation in the value of the business. Companies on a strong growth path with protective "moats" around their business are worth paying more for—Starbucks, anyone?

Segmented Portfolio

Construction of a segmented, or stratified, portfolio is an active investing fundamental. Each portfolio has different objectives and different sets of investments and investing styles. Segmentation produces focus; each investor can attend to the specific goals and tactics required by the portfolio. Beginning investors may not have enough "capital" to build out each of these portfolios to be large enough to be efficient, but as a thought process, the segmentation principle is important.

Foundation Portfolio

The foundation portfolio serves as the cornerstone of your total investment base. Foundation investments are primarily long term in nature and adjusted only infrequently. The main goal is to match market returns and to do so without consuming too much precious mindshare. Index funds, mutual funds, medium-term bonds, and TIPS (inflation-protected Treasury bonds) and solid long-term growth-oriented value stocks thus make sense for this portfolio. Stocks paying dividends are attractive, as such dividends have proven to be a significant portion of a stock's long term return.

Most of an active portfolio—perhaps 70 to 90 percent when starting out—is allocated to this base. Professional advice and management probably makes the most sense here. Retirement accounts, particularly 401(k)s, where investment options are limited already and monthly contributions add regularly to the base, comprise a large part of the foundation for many investors. Some investors may consider equity in their home as a bond surrogate and as part of their foundation—though it is inadvisable to use this base to justify shifting all other capital to more venturous investments.

Rotational Portfolio

The goal of this somewhat more active portfolio is to meet or slightly exceed market returns by staying ahead of changes in market and economic conditions. The rotational portfolio invests where the puck is going, generally by moving money to industry sectors or investment instruments coming into favor. Inflation scenarios favor industries producing raw materials or owning hard assets, real estate, and tend not to favor bonds or companies already under extreme competitive pressure. Downturns favor "defensive" sectors—food, suppliers of basic necessities, and some retailers. It is hard to truly stay in front of the pack, but over time, when armed with the right information, you should end up right more often than wrong. Exchange-traded funds (ETFs) are the simplest way to move capital among sectors. Professional advice may help here, particularly in interpreting economic and market signals, but watch for brokers and professional advisors who simply jump on bandwagons, usually too late.

Rotational investing takes some practice and long-term experience and may be the last—and smallest—of the three portfolios built by new active investors. Some rotational capability may exist in retirement and 401(k) accounts, depending on the breadth of funds and fund families offered, but it is important to verify that offerings truly reflect the sector—not just Microsoft, GE, and Exxon/Mobil with just a handful of truly sector-specific stocks.

Also watch for transaction costs, which can quickly delete the advantages of sector movement.

Opportunistic Portfolio

The opportunistic, "low-hanging fruit" portfolio is perhaps the most dynamic, exciting, and really fun part of the active portfolio. While it sounds a bit contrarian, the goal of this portfolio is really income, not growth. Active investors set aside a certain amount of capital—perhaps 10 or 20 percent of their portfolio in the beginning—to capture short-term trading gains, or better yet, with less risk, produce cash by selling covered call options. There are a lot of tools in this portfolio and each will take study and practice to get familiar with, but the "buy-write" covered call scenario is a good place to start. This portfolio has no set monthly or yearly objective; for having such would likely corner one into unfavorable investments. In fact, no activity in this (or any other) portfolio in a given month is just fine. But a covered call play can easily produce 3 to 5 percent and sometimes 10 percent returns in a month (36–120 percent per year, if *rolled over*, that is, repeated successfully). These types of short-term opportunities, when averaged across the portfolio, go a long way toward producing modestly above-market returns.

Opportunistic portfolios are typically set up in your taxable accounts with a certain amount of cash set aside, often using an active trading-oriented brokerage platform. Some stocks may be brought over from a foundation portfolio for the sake of providing coverage for covered call writing, but too much of this might excessively cap the foundation portfolio return. Some short-term swing trades may be achieved using margin, or borrowed funds, but it is most important to stay "within yourself" with these trades. Successful opportunistic investing requires setting objectives for each specific trade and harvesting the gains when

Putting Active Investing into Practice

achieved. Again, it may be contrarian thinking, but the opportunistic portfolio *must not* be driven by greed.

New active investors will probably want to get into this relatively cold pool a toe, a foot, a leg at a time. Practice through "paper"—that is, hypothetical—trading is a good idea. Hard work is required to select investments, and that hard work follows through to conclusion. Investments are monitored and sold with the same—or more—effort than went into their initial selection. Opportunistic investors keep close tabs on results and learn from mistakes. Finally, opportunistic investing takes a certain amount of tenacity, that is, willingness to continue through the odd failure. Tentative, confidence-lacking investing nearly always leads to failure.

Do It Yourself—Or Not

Along the way, active investors will repeatedly face the decision of whether to manage a portfolio—or part of a portfolio—themselves. The rule of thumb should probably be to "do it yourself" unless there's a good reason not to. "Good reasons" include (1) bandwidth and (2) expertise. Professional management—either in the form of professional fund managers or as personal financial advisors—should be considered if you don't have the time to manage all parts of a portfolio. Leaving a chunk of a foundation portfolio, like a 401(k) account, to others allows more time to focus on the opportunistic and rotational portfolios. Professional advisors and brokers—the right ones, anyway—can do some of legwork you would do with unlimited time.

Likewise, where expertise is lacking—as is normally true with international investments and may be true with small-cap stocks, commodities, and similar investments—professional help makes sense. Advisors with special expertise or research resources behind them should be considered.

The underlying themes are: (1) active investors should only consider advisors when the advisors can bring something to the table—time or expertise—that they don't have themselves, and (2) it must provide a favorable return on investment. That is, an advisor who charges large fees or is tied to large commissions is only worthwhile if the gains they achieve exceed their cost. Their track record should reflect these benefits, and it is worth asking, without naming names, for evidence that they have produced these kinds of gains for other investors. Benefit versus cost criteria should be tested before selecting any advisor, and your personal time should enter the equation.

Sizing Up Your Situation

It comes as no surprise that no two investors are alike. Each has a different personal financial situation, different objectives, and a different risk tolerance. Each formulates elements of their own situation into their investing strategy.

Tax Considerations

So far this book has not made much mention of taxes and tax consequences of different investing approaches. This important subject merits a few comments here.

Generally speaking, all investors should be willing to pay taxes, or, put another way, no investor should avoid income in order to avoid paying taxes. Taxed income is better than no income at all, so tax consequences in and of themselves shouldn't modify or marginalize investing activity. So for the most part, active investors should go about their business and not worry about tax effects.

That said, in practice (and it will come as no surprise) the complexity of today's tax system does add a few wrinkles. Most

Putting Active Investing into Practice

investors know that long-term capital gains are taxed at a lower rate, so gains that can be held for a year will face a smaller tax take. In fact, as Warren Buffett likes to point out, a gain that can be left on the table forever can never be taxed! For most of us, that truth doesn't apply, for we will all sell someday to achieve some other financial need, but another truth does apply: Money left to compound without an annual tax withdrawal will grow into a larger sum than funds diminished by yearly checks written to Uncle Sam (and his statehouse friends). Essentially, tax paid on realized gains, if one is in a 30 percent total tax bracket, will diminish an 8 percent annual gain into a 5.6 percent gain (8% * 70%), and the effect of diminished returns on compound growth was already illustrated in Chapter 2.

The effect of long-term growth and compounding should enter into the rational investor's decision to sell. In fact, like any sell decision, it's all about whether there is something better to buy, and the tax penalty becomes part of that decision. But to the contrary, a bird in hand is better than a loss later on, and a short-term investment producing desired results should be harvested and tax paid. Do it and move on. The Bush Administration 2003 ordinary income tax rate changes further reduce the impact of short-term sales.

Finally, tax-free investments in a taxable foundation portfolio account can make sense, and the new favorable dividend tax treatment make dividend-paying stocks more attractive. Bottom line: Taxes and your personal tax situation should be considered, but should not *govern* your active investing.

Risk Tolerance

Every investor has their own risk tolerance, usually shaped by overall personality and previous experience. Naturally, more risk-tolerant investors will make more risky plays particularly in the opportunistic portfolio and may have a larger opportunistic portfolio to begin with. But fundamentally, the active investing theme and premise applies to everybody. Many principles of active investing actually serve to diminish risk, and all but the least self-confident individuals will gain confidence as they get better at making rational investing decisions. That said, no investor should risk more than they are willing to lose, and any individual loss needs to be taken in context of the big picture. Your portfolio segmentation will necessarily reflect your risk tolerance, as will the investments selected for each portfolio. A balanced active portfolio should have gains somewhere; if not, you should take solace in the fact that even professionally managed funds are probably losing too. Like any craftsman or professional, you will make mistakes. But you should (1) size up what you did well; (2) credit yourself for the effort made to avoid mistakes; and (3) use the lessons learned to do better next time. All professionals work this way.

Learning By Example

Illustrations can help bring any written material to life, so let's take a look at a few hypothetical active investing examples. As you read them, notice not only the investment tools and vehicles that these people employ but also the lifestyles surrounding their active investing practices. It should be emphasized that these are only brief vignettes and are used as examples. They fall far short of representing comprehensive financial plans and are not intended as specific investment advice.

James Jameson

James Jameson is a single, twenty-seven-year-old retail information technology consultant who earns about $75,000 a year, traveling the country frequently to install systems and trouble-

Putting Active Investing into Practice 249

shoot problems. He travels about 60 percent of the time, and he can be in one place for a week or more, or sometimes just overnight. James has accumulated about $30K in a 401(k) plan that offers the usual assortment of funds, of which he has about 80 percent in aggressive growth funds and 20 percent in the shares of his own company. He has another $20K in individual IRAs and about $30K more to invest; he would like to eventually use this last amount to buy a home. His career path appears favorable, and his objectives are to grow his nonretirement savings fairly aggressively, while achieving at least market return with his retirement assets.

James makes a point of reading the *Wall Street Journal* at least twice a week (often on Monday morning and on Friday afternoon) while traveling. He reviews the latest economic numbers and keeps a list of investment prospects in his briefcase for more detailed review during down time, which may occur on weekends or a quiet evening on the road. If such a quiet evening occurs, he goes to the hotel "business center" and researches his investment choices through resources in the Yahoo!Finance portal. He also checks Yahoo!Finance each morning if possible, and calls "Telebroker" at least once a day to review quotes on his active stocks. When in the office, he checks Yahoo!Finance twice a day from his desk, and has his brokerage account set up to deliver him an e-mail alert any time his investments drop below or rise above a certain level.

Not surprisingly, James sees opportunity in retailers, particularly those ahead of the curve in deploying technology to make their operations more productive. He likes the "clean" operational model of CarMax, and also likes the new systematic category management activities being deployed at Borders Group, Inc. So he invests $10K in these companies in his "opportunistic" nonretirement portfolio and watches prices closely. The Borders position is fairly steady, and James knows he can sell it if his job ends or some other emergency arises. Occasionally, he has traded half of his position in CarMax as it bumped into the high and low of its trading range. Borders tends to be steadier, so he hasn't traded it, but he worries about Wal-Mart as a competitive threat. Finally, he deploys $15K of his IRA in SPDRs, occasionally rotating to cash when the S&P 500 gets close to its annual high. He continues to look for better rotational investments and is currently studying the list of ETF funds to identify a few that perform well during market downturns. Finally, he has a $5K hunch bet on Restoration Hardware—a concept retailer that could potentially benefit from systems improvements and is rapidly establishing a solid brand. Summary: James keeps steady track of everything and does opportunistic investing close to the industry he knows, while "leaving the driving to others" in his foundation portfolio.

Linda Lindberg

Linda is a forty-seven-year-old doctor and head of household earning about $150,000 per year. She is divorced and has primary custody of her two children. With about $300K in retirement assets and another $200K of nonretirement assets, her objectives are to (1) retire early to write books and (2) ensure her children get the best possible education. Some of the tactics she is considering include paying off her mortgage early and aggressively building the retirement portfolio. So Linda builds her foundation portfolio in two places: $200K of her $300K retirement assets are invested in a basket of funds chosen by a financial advisor, and $100K of her $200K nonretirement assets are invested in a "529" college savings plan. The 529 plan employs a blended strategy mixing bonds and stock investments, changing the allocation as her kids get older, so she doesn't have to manage this allocation herself.

Putting Active Investing into Practice

For the rest of her assets, Linda does most of her active portfolio management during her lunch hour, reviewing Yahoo!Finance and Briefing.com each day at lunch (the only time she feels any real "peace" during her day.) She does some rotational investing, mainly using ETFs in healthcare, energy, and retail fields with another $50K of her retirement portfolio. The rest of her retirement portfolio—$50K—and her nonretirement portfolio—$100K—is set aside for opportunistic investments. With this body of funds, Linda is in hot pursuit of cash returns; when successful, she adds at least part of her gains to her house payment to accelerate the mortgage payoff using her nonretirement opportunistic portfolio. She follows biotech stocks and buys a few like Imclone Systems for the purpose of writing covered calls. She owns 500 shares purchased at $48, and she sells $50 calls for about $3 each month—thus pocketing $1,500, which goes to the mortgage. When the stock closes with the option expiration period over $50, she looks for a re-entry point in the $40s. She also invests in the SPDR Biotech ETF, and she tracks recent developments in all biotech stocks in the news and by talking to others in her profession. She is also a believer in the eventual successful systematization of medical care, so she invests accordingly in WebMD, although she knows she will have to be patient with this one. Finally, she invests in Microsoft and in Johnson & Johnson, solid blue-chip names, which, in looking at cash flow and dividend policy, appear to be solid value investments more aligned to shareholder interests than most.

Although Linda has more to invest than James, many of the same principles are applied: stratified investments, a mix of short-term and long-term objectives, steadily monitoring business pulse, and looking for value in fields they know about.

Andrew Anderson

Mr. Anderson is a recently retired sixty-five-year-old insurance broker living with his also-retired wife in an "active seniors" community. He recently rolled his 401(k) plans over into directly controlled individual IRAs, and he has paid off his house. He has about $150K in additional investment funds outside of the retirement investments. His objective is to withdraw 4 percent per year ($1,000/month) from his retirement accounts to supplement the Social Security he and his wife receive to meet living expenses, and use any additional investment gains to fund travel and save for rainy days.

Having been burned in the 2000–2001 downturn by unreliable investment advisors and expensive, underperforming brokerage house mutual funds, Andrew still thinks fund investing makes sense, but he is now much more careful and wants to make his own choices. He is an avid reader of Morningstar mutual fund investment reports, and he screens funds with Morningstar and Yahoo!Finance mutual fund screening tools. He wants five-star funds in his portfolio and wants to pay 1 percent or less per year in fees—which is important for preserving his 4 percent annual withdrawals. He also stresses value in his investments, and he rarely pursues funds or stocks with anything other than a value perspective. He looks for individual companies with strong brands and steadily increasing profit margins in businesses he understands.

In pursuit of his 4 percent annual return, Andrew allocates his retirement assets as follows: 50 percent ($150K) is in ten-year Treasury bonds with staggered maturities yielding about 5 percent average overall. Because this return, after taxes, does not support his objective, other portfolio components are invested more aggressively, mainly in small- and mid-cap value-oriented funds and ETFs. He is not a big believer in his own ability to predict

Putting Active Investing into Practice 253

market cycles, but he sees the emerging shortage of petroleum refining capacity, combined with increasing demand, as an indicator of success with oil refiners such as Tesoro, Ashland, and Valero, so he has some rotational investments in this area, both in retirement and nonretirement assets. Once these stocks reach their full potential value, which he targets at 30 percent above current prices, he will sell them and probably buy some healthcare-related stocks and ETFs.

For opportunistic investments, Andrew still holds 1,000 shares of Starbucks that he purchased years ago. Although sitting on a handsome $35 per share profit, he still views the company as a long-term value play with a strong brand building international presence, and as a lasting and growing appeal to more segments of the population as a business and social gathering place. Not sure what to do, he regularly sells covered calls against half of this position, and with the recent surge in price above $45, would probably let the investment go if it were called away. This strategy can yield $500–$1,000 per month in extra income, which goes into the vacation fund. He enjoys movies and is a fan of the IMAX theater concept, and with the stock just above $5, considers it a turnaround with a strong brand and good value as the adoption of the format becomes more widespread internationally and domestically. He buys a few extra shares on dips and sells if they reach $5.50. He is currently looking for more plays like this.

Each day, Andrew gets *The New York Times* and the *Wall Street Journal* and watches things closely. He isn't comfortable with computers and the Internet, so he doesn't watch closely online. But he does go to the local library religiously—once a week, usually on Thursdays after the latest weekly Value Line reports arrive. Value Line is his main source of detailed investing information. He keeps a list of ideas, and he never invests in anything he finds in Value Line without taking at least a few days to think it over, drawing up his own pro-con scenario. He enjoys his investing, and staying active enough to feel in charge and achieve his objectives, but he is not so involved as to impart stress into the rest of his life.

Your Own Active Investing Style

As you develop and implement your own active investing program, you will have to take into account your lifestyle, family situation, amount of free time, base of knowledge, and long-term goals—just like the three people profiled above. No matter what flavor of active investing you choose, some common threads should run through it.

To sum up, the objective of active investing is *enhanced returns with reduced risk*. Active investors look to *modestly beat market returns while maintaining a margin of safety*. The active investing approach follows three basic tenets:

Blended Strategy:

- A mix of styles, tools, and approaches
- Versatile, adaptive, offensive and defensive
- A portfolio segmented into foundation, rotation, and opportunistic components
- Do-it-yourself and professional management

Rational Approach:

- Strong business rationale
- Enlightened by the best and most current information available
- Value oriented

Putting Active Investing into Practice

Modest Involvement:

- Aligned to busy lifestyle
- Not a full-time activity
- Inexpensive resources

Applied thoughtfully and consistently, such an active investing approach should help to give you and your family financial security and peace of mind today and in the future.

Index

A
accounting standards, 20–21
acquisition strategies, 133
active investing
    as blended style, 26, 240
    core principles of, 34–44
    vs. day trading, 152–154
    defined, viii–ix, 32–33
    examples of, 248–254
    objectives, 33–34, 240
    as rational investing, 42–43, 70, 241
    summary of, 44, 193–194, 239–245, 254–255
    time factor in, 31–32, 34
active traders, 75–76
asset allocation, 28–29, 39–41
asset preservation, 33
assets
    business, 124–126
    growth of, 34
auto sales, 88

B
balanced funds, 198
balance sheets, 114–115, 124–126
bear markets, 97–98
Black-Scholes model, 219
Bollinger bands, 176–177
bonds, 197–198, 234–236
brand value, 140
Briefing.com, 55, 59
brokerage services, 73–82
Buffet, Warren, vi, 26, 105
Business 2.0 (magazine), 62–63
business activity measures, 88–91
business appraisals, 113–145
    acquisition strategies and, 133
    debt and, 128–129
    financial statements and, 113–130
    investor benefit and, 130–133
    management and, 142–143
    ratio analysis, 134–138
    shares outstanding and, 129–130
    strategic intangibles and, 138–142
    value tests for, 116–130
business assets, 124–126
business cycles, 12, 18, 65–66, 96–99
business inventories, 89
BusinessWeek, 57
buy-and-hold approach, 26

C

call options, 220–224, 225–226
candlestick charts, 177–178
capital requirements, 118–120
cash flow statements, 115–120
charting, 79
Chicago Purchasing Managers Index (PMI), 90–91
closed-end funds, 196–197
CNBC, 55, 59
collective behavior, 167–168
commission deregulation, 5–6
commissions, 80
commodities, 95–96, 232–234
common stock funds, 197
company events, 164–167
company performance, 70
competitive profile, 139–140
confidence, crisis in, 19–21
construction measures, 91–93
construction spending, 92
consumer confidence, 67–68, 85
consumer credit, 85
consumer price index (CPI), 94–95
contrarian investing, 154
corporate governance, 20–21
corporate malfeance, 13–14, 20–21
cost-push inflation, 94
covered calls, 220–224

D

daily strength, 169–170
day trading, 27, 79–80, 150–154
debt, 128–129
defensive strategies
   bonds, 234–236
    commodities, 232–234
    options, 213–232

deflation, 93
demand-pull inflation, 93–94
deregulation, commission, 5–6
direct access, 80
discipline, 188
discount rate, 108, 109
disintermediation, 16
diversification, 29, 35, 236–237
dividends, 131
dollar cost averaging, 29–30
dot.com stocks, 11
doubling down, 187
durable goods, 89

E

earnings announcements, 164–165, 189
Earnings Before Taxes, Depreciation and Amortization (EBITDA), 123
economic cycles, 96–99
economic indicators, 65–68, 83–88
Economist, The, 57
Electronic Communications Networks (ECNs), 161
e-mail newsletters, 56, 59
employment cost index (ECI), 95
employment reports, 68, 85–86
entry barriers, 140–141
equity options, 132, 214–228, 231–232
exchange-traded funds (ETFs), 68–69, 193–195, 206–207, 211–212, 231–232
existing home sales, 92

F

factory orders, 89–90
financial advisors, 245–246

Index

financial market performance, 71–72
financial newspapers, 53
financial performance, predicting performance, 106–107, 110–111
financial portals, 53–55
financial services industry, 13–14, 19–21
financial statements, 113–130
  balance sheets, 114–115, 124–126
  cash flow statements, 115–120
  examples of, 116, 117, 121, 125
  income statements, 115, 120–124
financial strength ratios, 136
foreign investments, 7–8
foundation portfolios, 36, 39, 193–194, 242–243
funds
  balanced, 198
  bond, 197–198
  closed-end, 196–197
  common stock, 197
  costs of, 200–204
  exchange-traded funds (ETFs), 68–69, 193–195, 206–207, 211–212, 231–232
  holdings of, 206–207
  information sources for, 207–208
  management of, 207
  money market, 198
  mutual, 14, 21, 194–198
  open-ended, 196–198
  performance of, 199–200
  risks and, 204–205
  selecting, 208–210
  styles of, 198–199
  tax performance of, 200
  types of, 194–195
  unit investment trusts (UITs), 194, 210–211
future contracts, 232

G

globalization, 6–7, 17
government policies, 18
Graham, Benjamin, 105
gross domestic product (GDP), 86, 97
gross margin, 120, 122
growth, 109

H

half selling, 187–188
hedging, 213
home mortgages, 235
home prices, 92–93

I

income statements, 115, 120–124
index options, 229–231
industry indicators, 68–69
inflation, 6–7, 66, 93–96
information sources, 50–63
  Briefing.com, 55, 59
  Business 2.0, 62–63
  CNBC, 55, 59
  e-mail newsletters, 5659
  financial newspapers, 53
  financial portals, 53–55
  for funds, 207–208
  Internet and, 51–52
  Morningstar, 60–62
  Motley Fool, The, 62
  newsmagazines, 57

information sources (continued)
  Nightly Business Report (tv show), 56
  Value Line Investment Survey, 43, 57, 60
initial claims, 86–87
initial public offerings (IPOs), 166
insider knowledge, 167
interest rates, 6–8, 66
international investments, 236–237
international trade, 67, 87
Internet
  effect of, on investing, 16
  information sources on, 51–52
  online trading, 73–82
Internet stocks, 9–12
intrinsic value, 107–111
investing climate, changes in, 15–30
investing information. *See* information sources
investment opportunities, recognizing, 163–180
investment returns
  diminishing, 21–22
  rate of, v–viii, 23
investment strategies
  changing, 24, 26
  historical overview of, 4–14
  see also specific strategies
Investor's Business Daily, 53, 58

L

leading indicators index, 87
LEAPS (Long Term Equity Appreciation) contracts, 219
Level II quotes, 78–79
limit orders, 182–183

M

macro information, 65, 65–69
management fees, 202
management performance, 71, 142–143
manufacturing surveys, 90–91
margins, 81
market cycles, 96–99
market downturns, 42. *see also* defensive strategies
market events, 164–167
market orders, 182, 184–185
marketplace performance, 70–71
market presence, 138
market timing, 37
market volatility, 19
micro information, 65, 70–72
moats, 140–141
money market funds, 198
Morningstar, 60–62, 207
mortgages, 235
Motley Fool, The, 62
Moving Average Convergence Divergence (MACD), 179–180
moving averages, 170–172
mutual funds, 14, 21, 194–198. *see also* funds

N

naked calls, 222
NASDAQ
  arrival of, 5
  Level II quotes and, 78–79
  workings of, 157–160
National Association of Purchasing Managers (NAPM) survey, 90
net asset value (NAV), 196–197
net profit margin, 124
new home sales, 92–93

news, 77–78
newsmagazines, 57
newspapers, 53
New York Stock Exchange (NYSE), 155–157, 158, 160
New York Times, 53, 58
Nightly Business Report (tv show), 56, 59

O

online trading services, 73–82
open-ended funds, 196–198
operating expenses, 122–123
operating margin, 123–124
opportunistic portfolios, 38–39, 244–245
opportunity costs, 108
option chains, 218–229
options
    call, 220–226
    commissions on, 80
    equity, 132, 214–228
    on exchange traded funds, 231–232
    index, 229–231
    put, 224–227
    strategic use of, 227–228
    trading, 81, 219–227
    value of, 215–218
overcapitalization, 129–130

P, Q

peer plays, 166–167
Personal Consumption Expenditure (PCE), 88
Personal Income (PI), 88
portfolio segmentation, 35–39, 242
positioning, 138–139
pricing power, 141
producer price index (PPI), 95
productivity, 67, 126–128
productivity ratios, 135
professional management, of investments, 245–246
profitability ratios, 134–135
profits, 120
put options, 224–227
quotes, 77–79

R

ratio analysis, 134–138
rational investing, 42–43, 70, 241
Reagan, Ronald, 6–7
real estate activity, 91–93
real estate investment trusts (REITs), 210–211
real-time news/quotes, 77–78
recessions, 97–98
recovery, 98–99
regional manufacturing surveys, 90–91
relative strength, 169
research reports, 63
retail sales, 91
retirement accounts, 39
returns on investment, 106–107
risk, 109, 204–205
risk tolerance, 247–248
rotational portfolio, 36–38, 243–244

S

sales charges, 201–202
sector investing, 68–69, 189–190
segmented portfolios, 242
sell rules, 184, 185–188
sentiment indicators, 67–68

service economy, 16–17
share buybacks, 132–133
shares outstanding, 129–130
Sharpe's Ratio, 205
short selling, 186–187
short-term investing, 149–161, 163–180
Small Order Execution System (SOES), 158
spreads, 227
standard deviation, 204–205
statistical signals, 178–180
stock exchanges, 155–161
stock market
  declining trust in, 13–14
  government involvement in, 18
  history of, 4–14
  increased participation in, 17–18
  volatility, 19
stock options. *See* options
stock trading, 79–80, 155–161, 181–190
stop orders, 183–184
straddles, 227–228
strategic intangibles, 138–142
streaming news/quotes, 77–78
supply chain, 141–142
swing trades, 152–153, 189

T

tax considerations, 18–19, 200, 246–247
technical analysis, 168–180
technology, 9–12, 16
telephone trading, 80–81
10 percent rule, 184, 185
time factor, 31–32, 34
time value of money, 108
TIPS (Treasury Inflation Protection Security), 236

trade, international, 67, 87
trade balance, 87
trade executions, 79–80, 181–190
trading platforms, 73–82
trading ranges, 172–175, 189
Treasury bonds, 236
truck sales, 88
12-b-1 fees, 202

U

underperformance, 22–25, 203
unemployment statistics, 86–87
unit investment trusts (UITs), 194, 210–211
USA Today, 53, 58

V

valuation ratios, 136–137
value, intrinsic, 107–111
value investing, 27–28, 103–111, 143–144, 241–242. *see also* business appraisals
Value Line Investment Survey, 43, 57, 60
value tests, 116–130
VIX (Volatility IndeX), 231
volatility, 19

W

Wall Street Journal, 53, 58

Y

Y2K, 11–12
Yahoo!Finance, 53–54, 59, 79, 207–208